The Use and Misuse of Children

The Use and Misuse of Children

MOKOKOMA MOKHONOANA

sekoala
PUBLISHING COMPANY (PTY) LTD

sekoala
PUBLISHING COMPANY (PTY) LTD

Mokokoma Mokhonoana,
Copyright © 2017.

ISBN: 978-0-9947212-0-4 (Hardcover)
ISBN: 978-0-9947212-1-1 (Paperback)
ISBN: 978-0-9947212-2-8 (eBook)

Cover design: Mokokoma Mokhonoana
Book design: Mokokoma Mokhonoana

Sekoala Publishing Company (Pty) Ltd

www.sekoala.com

The Use and Misuse of Children

CONTENTS

INTRODUCTION

I would not be surprised if this book eventually earns its author one of the top spots on the list that is made up of the names of the most hated human beings, and if it eventually earns itself one of the top spots on the list that is made up of the names of the most depressing books. As we all know, some facts about life, some facts about some human beings, and some facts about all human beings are depressing. What's more, the average sane human being is likely to hate you if you intentionally make them think about depressing facts that they have chosen to ignore or forget, and/or those that they did not know, especially if they cannot do anything to change them; or if they are under the impression that they cannot.

Indeed, this book is in a way an exploration of the purpose of human life. While it is obviously about everybody, this book is definitely not for everybody. It goes without saying that it is about everybody because, whether or not they are a parent or they want to be one, every human being is or was a child. And it is not for everybody not because not everybody can read but because not everybody who can read has the stamina that is required to read a book that not only makes one realize or remember some unpleasant facts about life, some disheartening facts about some human beings, and some depressing facts about all human beings but also shatters some of the countless comforting misbeliefs and lies that we sane human beings tell each other about life and some or all human beings.

In addition to that, this book is boring. Or rather, most of the people who will read this book will find it boring. And that is, among other reasons, because, unlike many writers whose books are deemed interesting by most of their readers, I am not about to tell the reader that some or all human beings are great. As a matter of fact, among other things, I am about to demonstrate that some of the adverse effects that some people's use of some people has had on some people are great.

In the nature of things, most of this book's readers will not like it, and that includes those who will have had the mental stamina that is required to read this book in its entirety. But that is not necessarily a bad thing, nor does it make this book useless. As we all know, many a person's health was improved, and many a person's life was saved, by the operation or medication that they did not enjoy.

As far as I can see, this book will positively impact the most people who are still not sure whether or not they want to be parents someday, people who have the desire to forever remain non-parents but lack the courage to do so, people who want to but cannot have children, people who are physically disabled, people who are parents, people whose children are physically or mentally disabled, and people who plan on being parents someday. One of the things that I knew before I even started writing this book is that it will definitely increase the number of people who will choose not to have children. And one of the things that I did not know about it when I started writing it is that it would end up as a book that is way more likely to transform some of its readers into good or better parents than many if not most parenting books, even though it is not really about parenting.

While ignorance is definitely bliss, being ignorant of some things is deadly. In their never-ending endeavours to remain or seem like good parents, millions of parents, for example, are unknowingly poisoning their own children. In other words, those parents are unknowingly increasing their chances of having to bury their own children someday. In addition to unknowingly not only allowing but also helping some people to slowly poison their children, those parents thank those people by repeatedly giving them some of their hard-earned money.

What I have just said is, needless to say, a non-arrogant way of asserting that hundreds of thousands if not millions of people who used to be alive would be alive if their parents had read this book.

The following exploration of the use and misuse of children is divided into three main parts: (1) "The Idea of Childhood," which revolves around and is a humble attempt of mine to summarize a thought-provoking book by Neil Postman; (2) "The Natural Use of Children," a very short chapter that touches on what seems to me to be the main things that Mother Nature achieves through children; and (3) "The Human Use of Children," which is made up of many of my convictions with regard to why and how we sane human beings use children.

Finally, with this book, I, like many a social critic, play the role of a mirror not that of a dietician, a surgeon, or a beautician. But that does not necessarily make this book useless. I mean, many if not most of the people who once used the services of a dietician, a surgeon, or a beautician would not have done that if they had never used a mirror. What's more, a mirror is valuable even in instances where the blemish that it has revealed cannot be removed or concealed, because such a revelation increases the number of things that one knows about oneself.

PART I:
THE IDEA OF CHILDHOOD

The origin of *The Disappearance of Childhood*, the book that I am about to attempt to summarize, is in Neil Postman's observation that childhood is disappearing, that the dividing line between adulthood and childhood is being destroyed, and at dazzling speed. Since he believed that that is self-evident, he focused not on giving substance to that but on enlightening the reader as to the origin of the idea of childhood and on the reason why it should be disappearing.[1]

When writing that book, Postman was of the controversial conviction that childhood is an idea (which he attributes to the Renaissance), a social artifact, a product of man's mind, a social construct, not a biological category like infancy, that "our genes contain no clear instructions about who is and who is not a child," and that a distinction between the world of a child and the world of an adult is not required for the survival of young human beings. In the nature of things, he was of the unshakable belief that a culture can exist without a social idea of children.[2]

To substantiate that, Postman reminds the reader that: one, the custom of celebrating the birthday of a child did not exist in America throughout most of the eighteenth century, and the cultural habit of precisely marking the age of a child is relatively new ("no more than two hundred years old")[3]; and, two, only seven percent of the children who were not only between the ages of fourteen and seventeen but also living in America in 1890 were enrolled by American high schools (the other ninety-three percent and many children who were much younger worked at adult labour, some of them worked from sunup to sundown).[4]

Because he was an avid student of general semantics, Postman tells the reader, before the reader reaches the very last sentence of the very first paragraph of his book's introduction, what he means by the word *children*. In the book in question, he has used the word *children* to refer to a special category of human beings who (1) are somewhere between the ages of seven and seventeen; (2) are generally believed to be qualitatively different from adults; and (3) are in need of special kinds of nurturing and protection.[5]

The Disappearance of Childhood is divided into two parts: "The Invention of Childhood," which Postman has dedicated to showing the reader the origin of the idea of childhood, and "The Disappearance of Childhood," which he has devoted to showing the reader why the present-day communication environment has made the idea of childhood not only difficult to sustain but also no longer relevant.

The Invention of Childhood

At the heart of Neil Postman's exploration, as far as I can see, lies the juxtaposition of the communication environment of the Middle Ages (which made childhood as we know, or rather *knew*, it impossible) and the communication environment of the era during which he has published his book (which wasn't that different from the communication environment of the era during which I have published this book). By *communication environment* he, I believe, refers to the thing or things that members of a culture use to communicate with each other; that is to say, the form or forms of human communication, spoken and/or written, together with the tool or tools with which they transmit whatever it is that they want to communicate.

According to Postman, Europe's descent into what is known as the Dark and then the Middle Ages, which began with the fall of the Roman Empire, led to the disappearance of literacy, the disappearance of education, and the disappearance of shame, which, as an inevitable result, has led or is leading to the disappearance of childhood.[6]

Let us touch on shame before we touch on literacy and education.

In a word, the culture in question lacked two things that make the idea of shame possible, namely, an ability and willingness to hide some things from children, and the concept of what we call manners. In the nature of things, medieval people, for example, were not, according to Postman, shamed by the exposure of their own bodily functions in front of others[7]; and the practice of playing with children's genitals, according to Phillippe Aries, formed part of a widespread tradition, which, as Postman reminds the reader, will get one up to thirty years in prison today.[8]

After the fall of the Roman Empire, the use of the Roman alphabet contracted to the point where social literacy, a condition where most people can and do read, was replaced by the condition that had preceded it, namely, craft literacy, a condition where the art of reading is restricted to a few people who inevitably form a privileged class.[9] (In the book in question, a literate culture is defined on the basis of how many members of the culture can read, and how easily, not on the basis of its having a writing system.) In other words, the Roman alphabet did not disappear; most Europeans' capacities to interpret it did.[10] Naturally, important social interactions were conducted face to face, by word of mouth, and most people acquired knowledge mainly through their ears, which means that Europe went back to a "natural" condition of human communication, which was dominated by speech and reinforced by song, seeing that, according to Postman, our genes are programmed for spoken language, which, unlike literacy, is certainly not a product of cultural conditioning.[11]

It is, I believe, necessary for me to remind readers who are of an opposing conviction that, in addition to observation, the vast majority of children who can talk have learned to talk from the mere act of listening, which obviously happens naturally, but, while reading can definitely make one a better writer, no human being can learn to write by merely looking at written or printed material and/or by observing people read or write; writing, like reading, has to be taught to them.

Anyway, the knowledge or the ignorance of cultural secrets, as far as I can see, is, according to Postman, one of the main differences between an adult and a child; the adult knows some facts and some facets of life—its tragedies, its contradictions, its violence, etc.—that are not regarded as suitable for children to know.[12] An unnatural method of human communication was needed to create and then sustain that difference. That is, of course, where literacy came in. Literacy, in a word, makes it possible for a culture to hide its secrets behind the printed word, which, needless to say, one cannot see unless one was taught to read.

In the sixteenth century, the invention of the printing press, which took place around the middle of the fifteenth century, and the resurrected social literacy, a condition where most people can and do read, led to the formation of a new communication environment, which finally made it possible for that culture to dramatically increase the average number of years that it took its children to discover, or rather uncover, its secrets. A new definition of adulthood *based on the ability to read*, and a new conception of childhood *based on the inability to read*, was created by the printing press.[13] In other words, in the literate world that eventually followed the invention of the printing press, children had to learn to read in order to *earn* adulthood by uncovering and accumulating secrets of their culture in stages.

Because no intervening stage was needed at the time, before the printing press created the new communication environment, *adulthood began as soon as infancy ended at seven.* (Why seven? *Because children have command over speech at that age*). Even if it were needed, creating the intervening stage we call childhood was impossible during the era that preceded the period in question, because, in addition to literacy and the idea of shame, that era lacked primary schools and, as a result, a sharp distinction between the world of adults and the world of children. Indeed, it lacked the former because there is no need for such schools where communication competence is determined by biology.[14]

Needless to say, the new adulthood, to which literacy was a ticket, excluded children. A new world was then needed for them to inhabit as they were expelled from the world of adults. That world was created and is known as childhood.[15]

The Disappearance of Childhood

Before the communication environment that was eventually brought about by the invention of the printing press together with the resurrected social literacy, there was no need for and a way to create and then sustain the idea of childhood as a social structure, because all members of medieval society shared the very same information environment and thus lived in the same intellectual and social world.[16]

The primary role of the second and last part of Neil Postman's exploration, which focuses exclusively on America, is, as far as I can see, to show the reader why and how electric media and what Daniel Boorstin has called the "graphic revolution" (that is, the emergence of a symbolic world of pictures, advertisements, posters, and cartoons[17]) have led to a communication environment that is akin to the communication environment that existed between the fall of the Roman Empire, which had led to Europe's regression from social to craft literacy, and the communication environment that was brought about by the invention of the printing press together with the resurrected social literacy, a relatively new communication environment that has made childhood as a social structure not only difficult to sustain but also no longer relevant. Indeed, that communication environment, which is only slightly different from the present-day communication environment of America, is the side effect of the assault on language and literacy by the

11

electric and graphic revolutions.[18]

Before we focus on the impact that television has had on America's ability to keep its children ignorant of the information that it does not deem suitable for them to know, let us touch on the division of sane human beings into groups based on the exclusivity of the information that they possess and/or are regularly fed.

Many a group is, according to Postman, largely defined by the exclusivity of the information that is shared by its members. There would be no lawyers, if we all knew what lawyers know. There would be no need to differentiate between teachers and their students, if the latter knew what the former know. And there would be no point to having grades, if third-graders knew everything that ninth-graders know.[19] That is at the heart of Neil Postman's argument. The same can, of course, be said about the two groups in question, namely, children and adults. In short, it is pointless to put young human beings into a group called children, if, for example, nine-year-olds know pretty much everything that ninety-year-olds know.

Let us now touch on the impact that television,

which Postman regarded as the coming together of the electric and graphic revolutions, has had on the communication environment that made childhood possible.

The assumption that, say, first-graders, do not yet know the information and the ideas that are fed to, say, twelfth-graders, could be rationally made in a print-based culture because (1) the printed word is sufficiently difficult to master that while a third-grader who is able to read effortlessly might be able to read most of the sentences that are found in an eleventh grade textbook, he or she will probably not *understand* most of them; which means that, for many if not most children, having access to a book that contains information that is not regarded as suitable for children to know is not enough for them to see the information that is hidden behind the words in it, *even if they can read with ease*; and (2) the literate attitude, which requires things such as quietness, contemplation, immobility, patience, and concentration, is sufficiently difficult to achieve. Naturally, the printed word and the literate attitude were an effective barrier between adults and children, even between young children and adolescents.[20]

According to Postman, television, because it is first and foremost a visual medium, has collapsed that information hierarchy. Postman asserted that, even though language is heard on television, and sometimes assumes importance, it is the picture that not only carries the critical meanings but also has a commanding influence on the viewer's consciousness.[21] And, because there are no ABCs for images, one's effort to learn to interpret the meaning of images—unlike one's endeavour to learn to interpret the meaning of words and sentences—need not be preceded by lessons in grammar or logic or vocabulary or spelling.[22] Indeed, that is why Postman was of the conviction that a six-year-old and a sixty-year-old are equally qualified to experience what television has to offer.[23]

In a nutshell, television images carry the critical meanings, and, as an inevitable result, because watching television and interpreting the meaning of its images do not require skills, the vast majority of information that is transmitted via television is available to and is understood by the vast majority of Americans.

It goes without saying that the undeniable fact that

the vast majority of Americans could interpret the meaning that were carried by television images was certainly not enough to choke the idea of childhood to death. Indeed, that alone would not have led to the suffocation of the idea of childhood if everybody who profited from American television before and during the period in question believed and, more importantly, avoided making television programs that conflict with the belief that some things are just too shameful and/or not fit to be shown and/or discussed on television, because not every American who watched (and made sense of the information that they were fed via) television was an adult.

As one would expect, television requires novel and interesting information in order for it to attract and, equally important, keep our attention, which is almost always sold to advertisers. In the nature of things, gazillions of people who make television programs make and/or used to make programs on homosexuality, abortion, incest, promiscuity, premature ejaculation, infertility, and other secrets of adult life. What's more, some secrets of adult life are, of course, unwittingly and prematurely revealed to children by advertisers. Needless to say, because of television's inability to effectively segregate its audience, many a television advertisement for things such as disposable sanitary pads and panty liners, for example, is seen by millions of girls ... and boys ... every single time it is aired.

To sum up, the lack of a means for adults to know exclusive information is, according to Postman, the reason why there were no children in the Middle Ages. The communication environment that was brought about by the invention of the printing press and the resurrection of social literacy made it possible for adults to know exclusive information; until that was made impossible again after electric media, especially television, had assaulted language and literacy.[24] Indeed, the electric media's disclosure of the entire content of the adult world had profound consequences such as the dilution and demystification of the idea of shame,[25] which is, of course, a mechanism by which we sane human beings keep barbarism at arm's length. And the idea of shame, according to Postman, is one of the things that make the idea of childhood possible, and is also unable to function effectively as a means of role differentiation in a society that is unable to keep secrets.[26]

Finally, clothing is one of the things that Postman has used to give substance to his main conviction. In short, because children shared the very same symbolic world with adults and were therefore seen as "miniature adults," during the Middle Ages size, as far as I can see, was the only visible difference between the clothes that children wore and the clothes that were worn by adults; and style was added to size as soon as the then new communication environment led to the invention of a then new world called childhood. However, the death of the idea of childhood, which Postman has attributed to the present-day communication environment, which was created by electric media together with graphic revolutions, has taken or is taking Americans to a situation that is similar to the Middle Ages with regard to clothing, a situation where size is the only visible difference between the clothes that are worn by, say, a nine-year-old girl, and the clothes that are worn by, say, a twenty-nine-year-old woman, when, needless to say, the girl is not at school and the woman is not at work.

If Postman's Book Were Written Today

It goes without saying that what Neil Postman has said about the then present-day America could be said about many if not most countries at that time; and the same can be said about all of those countries today. It also goes without saying that Postman's book, because of the period during which it was written, does not discuss communication technologies such as the internet, social media, and smartphones, which are, I believe, as destructive as if not more destructive than television with regard to their impact on a society's ability to keep its children ignorant of information that it does not regard as suitable for children to know.

Because of that, I would like to conclude this attempt of mine to summarize his book by sharing four instances that each left me thinking about his book.

Instance number one: I once came across, on Twitter, a photo of a boy who looked about three years old smooching, on a couch, a baby girl who looked about eighteen months old. The boy clasped his right arm around the poor girl's back while he was either pulling her towards himself with his left hand, or holding her right hand with his left hand to make it even more difficult for her to escape his grasp. Like the baby girl, who was wearing a nappy and long socks, he was topless. His eyes were closed. And his tiny lips were sucking her bottom lip and the tip of her tongue while her mouth was wide open because she was crying.

For the second instance, I will simply cite a question that a girl whose Facebook profile claimed that she was thirteen years old at that time—and whose then recently shot profile picture left me with the impression that she was one or two years younger than that—asked on some Facebook group that is or was then used by its members to discuss sexual matters: "Guys, what is an orgasm?"

Third instance: Six or so months ago, I, for almost a minute, had access to a smartphone that belonged to girl who was eleven at that time. Because I was writing this part of this book, which is an attempt to summarize Postman's book, the very first thing that I did was glance at the pictures that I found on her phone. I was, if truth be told, looking for pictures that I would use to support some of Postman's convictions. I did not find any. And I was a bit disappointed but very happy that

I did not. After that, I returned her phone. But I still had an unshakable feeling that she had such pictures hidden somewhere on her phone. That is probably because she kept on hurrying me while I was searching her phone for such pictures—she thought I was reading the sweet nothings that her boyfriend had recently sent to her via WhatsApp. Anyway, I, after a few minutes, managed to convince her to lend me her phone again so I can "reread" the messages from her boyfriend. A few minutes later, after searching wherever I could that I did not search the first time, I found a folder that I did not see when I was secretly browsing her pictures. After glancing at the first eighteen or so pictures of Barbie dolls, smartphones, other toys, and female clothes, which were all in the folder in question, I finally found two pictures that support some of Postman's convictions. The first is of a woman and a man whose erect penis is swallowed by the woman's shaven vagina. And the second is of a man's hairy scrotum inside a woman's hand, and his erect penis inside the woman's mouth.

Fourth and last instance: A video went viral in South Africa a few weeks ago. In the video, which she apparently shot for her boyfriend, a girl who looks and is said to be fourteen years old says something to what seems to be the camera of a smartphone, becomes completely naked after taking off her Hello Kitty pyjamas, and then masturbates; first with a tiny dildo, and then with her small fingers.

(Needless to say, that instance substantiates my belief that the internet, social media, and mobile devices such as tablets and smartphones are probably more destructive than television with regard to the impact they have on a society's ability to keep its children ignorant of information that it does not regard as suitable for them to know, owing to the undeniable fact that those relatively new communication technologies, unlike television, also make it possible for us—adults *and children*—to produce words, images, and videos that reveal that kind of information, and to instantly send them to hundreds, thousands, or even millions of people with ease and without having to pay for advertising space.)

PART II:
THE NATURAL USE OF CHILDREN

As the alert reader is about to notice, in many if not most of the instances where I will use the name "Mother Nature," which—as we all know—is a common personification of nature, I will be referring to whoever or whatever that has created and is now the "ruler" of the universe. I hope that the reader is aware that that does not necessarily mean that I attribute to nature the creation of everything that exists except man-made things. And that it is people, not words, that mean; that is to say, words are nothing but empty vessels that people fill with meaning.

It goes without saying that one of the words that this book's title is made up of—the word *misuse*—implies that there is at least one right way of using children. I have, if truth be told, absolutely no idea if there is such a thing as a right way of using a child. Heck, I don't even know if there really is a right way of using a human being. Having said that, I am well aware that one can, with reason, regard the way in which children are used by nature as *a* if not *the* right way of using children, owing to the fact that, one, children were, are, and will in all likelihood always be made by Mother Nature (like I once quipped, "human beings cannot really make a baby; they can only make love"), and, two, Mother Nature, unlike us human beings, has been using children to achieve the very same objective or objectives ever since the birth of the world's very first child.

One of the things that the vast majority of human beings are unlikely if not unable to do with their minds is, I believe, to accept the undeniable fact that life can go on without the existence of human beings. That is sort of understandable because, as we all know, there is no video that shows and there were no human beings—not even one human being—to witness life go on without the existence of human beings before the birth or the creation of the world's very first human being.

Apart from the fact that before the existence of human beings there were no human beings to see life go on without human beings, it is unlikely if not impossible for most sane human beings to accept the fact that life can go on without us human beings, owing to the fact that, needless to say, they, in the nature of things, were each left by their or somebody else's interpretation of some religious texts with the preposterous belief that human beings are the central or most important element of existence—that life revolves around human beings, despite the undeniable fact that Mother Nature treats human beings the very same way that She treats animals. (I believe that, if truth be told, life does not revolve around human beings; the average human life revolves around being.)

In the nature of things, the now unshakable belief that we human beings are the most important element of existence has left most sane human beings arrogant. Although I, like a relatively small number of people, know that nothing is as irritating as someone who brags about their modesty, I am going to risk coming across as bragging about my humility by asserting that I am definitely not arrogant, and that is because, one, I, as the reader has just found out, do not buy the claim that life revolves around human beings, and, two, I, as the reader is about to find out, do not suffer from an exaggerated sense of my own abilities.

Like each and every human being, I am unable to uncover the real reason why Mother Nature has brought human beings into existence. (Or to prove that what most sane human beings believe to be the real reason is the real reason. If it is the real reason, that is.) Because of that fact, which most readers will readily label as an opinion so that they will still be able to retain the belief that their lives are each way more important to Mother Nature than the life of each and every animal and the life of every single plant, I will not write as if I do. I will, instead of doing that, share a few observations of mine, which, needless to say, were heavily molded by things such as my very limited senses, experience, and knowledge.

Although we will never know if the same can be said about life, because we were absent before life's birth and will definitely be absent after life's death if death awaits life, we know without a shadow of a doubt that living things are subject to the cycle of life and death, and that there is, between life and death, a process called growth. In other words, life implies growth and death. As we all know, you cannot live without growing, and you cannot grow without dying.

To come to the point, before many an impatient reader accuses me of beating around the bush, children are nothing but seeds with which Mother Nature patiently attempts to make adults. And the primary if not the only function of adults is—or at least seems to me to be—to produce children. To Mother Nature, that is. Obviously, that is misleading because, as we all know, being an adult is not a prerequisite for becoming a parent. (It goes without saying that that undeniable fact gives substance to some of the aforementioned convictions that are attributed to Neil Postman by the cover of *The Disappearance of Childhood*.)

Needless to say, because She does not have the concept of waste like we human beings do, Mother Nature, in many if not most of the cases where She has just failed to transform a child into an adult, uses children's bodies to feed Her other children, some

29

of whom we refer to with the word *worms*. I am, of course, referring to instances where, because of the failure in question, he who is nearby and not deaf is a billion times more likely to hear the phrase "gone too soon," which was probably first said by someone who was then unwilling to accept the undeniable fact that death devours not only those who have been cooked by old age; it also feasts on those who are half-cooked and even those who are raw.

Indeed, feeding children's bodies, or any corpse for that matter, to worms makes Mother Nature seem cruel and unfair to many if not most sane human beings. But that is, I believe, only because they have never realized or they have forgotten that during our pitiful recurrent endeavours to evade starvation we human beings have killed countless trillions and continue to kill innumerable millions of Mother Nature's other children whom we call animals and plants. I think, if truth be told, (the kind of) worms (in question) are not as cruel as, or rather cruel like, human beings and many of Mother Nature's other children because, unlike us and them, (the kind of) worms (in question) seldom, if ever, kill to avoid starving to death. Having said that, one can, needless to say, defend our recurrent killing of other living things by simply mentioning the undeniable fact that it is Mother Nature who gave us the fear of death and thus the desire to live forever or at least for as long as we possibly can, and that, because of how She has made us, we cannot succeed in our recurrent endeavours to continue to live without eating things that have just failed in their endeavours to continue to live.

PART III:
THE HUMAN USE OF CHILDREN

Unlike the last part, this last part of the book is, needless to say, not made up of the use of children by Mother Nature, and that is the only reason why it is way longer than the last part. For no reason other than for the sake of orderliness, this third and last part is divided into the following parts: (1) The Use of Children by Society; (2) The Use of Girls by Men; (3) The Use of Children by Companies; (4) The Use of Children by Children; (5) The Use of Children by Adults; (6) The Use of Children by Grandparents; (7) The Use of Children by Parents; (8) The Ideal Human Being; (9) Abortion, Suicide, Homosexuality, and Masturbation; (10) Childless versus Childfree; (11) Antinatalism; (12) Childlessness and Selfishness; and (13) Negative Reviews of a Product Called Child.

It goes without saying that I would have still been able to explore the very same subjects and to say the very same things if I had divided this part of the book into fewer parts. And that is, of course, because all parents, for example, are part of a society, and, in many if not most societies, many if not most parents are each part of at least one company; and companies, as we all know, use their employees during their endeavours to provide and/or to produce whatever services and/or products that all or some people need, or, as it is the case in many a case, services and/or products that their shareholders want all or some sane people to want.

Two other facts that are as plain as the nose on the reader's face (or my face if the reader does not have a nose) but are worth mentioning nonetheless are that: (1) we human beings of today do not use children to achieve some of the things that all or some of the people who were children when my great-great-great-great-great-great-great-great-great-grandparents were children were used to achieve; and (2) some of the ways that we human beings of today use children would definitely be deemed not only bizarre but also distasteful by any randomly selected sane adult that was born centuries ago, if we were to somehow do to their corpse, or rather skeleton, what is believed by most Christians to have been done to Jesus Christ's corpse three days and three nights after he was crucified.

The Use of Children by Society

As Margaret Thatcher is said to have reminded us, there is, of course, no such thing as society. As we all know, you cannot really see or destroy society, you can only see or destroy "the aggregate of [individuals] living together in a more or less ordered community" or "the community of [individuals] living in a particular country or region and having shared customs, laws, and organizations" or "the totality of people regarded as forming a community of interdependent individuals."

Like I did in the previous part of this book with nature and whatever or whoever to whom the creation of the universe is attributable, I will, in this very last part of this book, personify society. What's more, I will, as an attempt to minimize confusion, capitalize the pronouns with which I will be referring to society. Obviously, doing that would be confusing if I refer to society as a male, since that is how many if not most of the people who will read this book will have been conditioned to refer to God whenever they use a pronoun to refer to Him.

Indeed, I had to make known what I have just made known with the previous sentence, because—thanks to the kind of picture of society that I am about to paint while referring to society as a she—many a reader would have definitely been left under the impression that I am a misogynist if I had not touched on that. Granted, a few women and girls have each broken my heart many times, and, before I decided to want only women who want me, a few women who I wanted did not want me, but I do not hate women. That is, by the way, what I told my parents two years ago just after they have read the following aphorism of mine from a book of aphorisms that I had just published, "A vagina is an uneducated woman's diploma." Believe it or not, I had to defend myself again, when my parents accused me of being a misogynist for the second time, two weeks ago just after I had published the following aphorism of mine, "Size definitely counts: some vaginas are just too big." But I am hopeful that they will someday be forced to swallow their words if and when they come across the following aphorism of mine, "Making God a man is the consolation prize that our forefathers have given themselves for not being the ones who were each blessed with a vagina."

Anyway, enough about (some of) my convictions with regard to the muscular tube leading from the external genitals to the cervix of the uterus in women.

There is, of course, a similarity between Mother Nature and Society: both are forever moving heaven and earth to prevent extinction. Having said that, there is a relevant difference between them with regard to their never-ending endeavours to prevent extinction. In a word, Mother Nature is mainly concerned with the prevention of the extinction of Her own children, whereas Society is mainly concerned with the prevention of Her own extinction. Fortunately for us human beings, because She is made up of nothing but human

beings, Society needs us because without our existence She cannot prevent Her own extinction. However, unfortunately for us, She needs only a few of us in
order for Her to achieve that selfish goal of Hers.

In order to make it not only possible but also effort-
less for Her to frequently lure us into having sexual intercourse, which sometimes leads to the only process
with which She is forever trying to make more of us,
Mother Nature has blessed and cursed pretty much
all fertile human beings with the ability to be sexually excited and the ability to experience that fleeting
yet sought-after thing called an orgasm (that is, by the
way, what inspired me to pen the following aphorism,
"If ejaculation weren't accompanied by an orgasm
chances are that the human population would have
never reached a billion ... or even a million"). Having said that, Mother Nature continues to dismally
fail to make as many human beings as humanly possible because gazillions of us sane human beings each
make that impossible by using a contraceptive before
or during some or all of our frequent endeavours to
bring about at least one orgasm, by realizing the cli-
max of sexual excitement through masturbation, and/

or by giving rise to an orgasm or orgasms by sleeping with a person or people who, like us, have fallopian tubes or testicles.

It goes without saying that as omnipotent as Mother Nature is or seems to be, once in a while She fails to prevent the extinction of one of Her offspring. If creatures such as dodoes, dinosaurs, and woolly mammoths once existed like we are told by many a paleontologist, that is. Speaking of extinction, I am not and I will definitely never be dead sure, but I strongly believe that it is pretty much impossible for someone or something to kill Mother Nature. As a matter of fact, as omnipotent as She is or seems to be, even She cannot kill Herself. Having said that, it is, as we all know, quite possible for someone or something to kill Society, and for Society to kill Herself.

Needless to say, many a thinking person has asked and continues to ask themselves (and those who care to listen to them) the following question, "Why the hell does Mother Nature keep on replacing Her dead and Her dying offspring with newborns?" I, if truth be told, have absolutely no idea, but I suspect that She is using all living things as nothing but entertainment, probably because She, like pretty much all sane human beings, is terrified of boredom and loneliness.

Anyway, in order for Her to realize the prevention of Her own extinction, which is without a doubt Her primary goal, Society—in addition to a few other tasks—has to continue to minimize the number of human deaths that were caused by other human beings, and to maximize the number of fertile human beings who will each be a parent come the day during which they will finally exit the land of the living.

Let us start with the first task. It goes without saying that for Her endless endeavour to minimize the number of human deaths that are each attributable to a human being or human beings, Society uses the law, which, to stand a chance of being effective, desperately needs the vast majority of sane human beings to believe that it is so much easier for an individual to survive when they are part of a community, that a teenager who is part of a community will in all likelihood outlive a teenager who lives alone on or as an island (apart from humans' being social beings, the vast majority of sane human beings—in the nature of things—find being part of a community desirable because they want to live for as long as they can, since they have realized that they cannot live forever like they want to).

I mean, most if not all members of most communities each stands a better chance of not being killed by an animal or animals, because being part of a community means that we are not as close to deadly animals as we would have been if we each lived alone as an island, plus some members of our communities are likely to be there to help us should we find ourselves being attacked by such an animal. (Obviously, that will seem like an unnecessary advantage to many a reader. But that's only because, thanks to their being part of a community, most civilized people have never come across wild animals that would have readily attempted to kill them and then use their corpses to evade starvation ... or to please their, the animals', tongues.) Having said that, one can, of course, argue, with reason, that innumerable millions of human beings would not have been killed by human beings if they had not been part of a community. What's more, hundreds of thousands if not millions of people were each killed by an animal or animals that would not have killed them if they had not visited or worked at a zoo or a game reserve (which would have definitely never existed if each and every person lived alone as an island) if human beings had never formed communities.

Finally, let us now touch on the other task, that is, Society's never-ending endeavour to maximize the number of human beings who will have each made at least one child or, preferably, as many children as they possibly could have made come the day they are going to kick the bucket. With the help of at least one fertile human being who—unlike them—has a cervical canal or a scrotum, that is.

As I have already asserted, because She is terrified of death like many if not most animals and pretty much all sane human beings, Society's life revolves around Her never-ending endeavour to prevent Her own death. (As I once asserted through an aphorism of mine, "The continuation of man's life is more attributable to his fear of death than it is to his desire to live. As a matter of fact, in countless cases, it is attributable to only the former.") Anyway, this task is, of course, made a trillion times easier than the other task by the fact that every now and then Mother Nature, because She is forever striving to produce more human beings, makes us sexually excited in order for Her to dramatically increase Her chances of dramatically decreasing the number of fertile human beings who will each still not be a parent on the day that they are going to meet their death.

Indeed, my implicit conviction that Mother Nature is obsessed with making as many children as it is humanly possible is, of course, given substance by the undeniable fact that She readily allows, to fall pregnant, many a woman and many a girl whose intent was not to reproduce when they each had sex with at least one fertile man or boy, many a woman and many a girl who are each not mentally and/or financially ready to be a parent, many a woman and many a girl who are mentally ill, and, perhaps more saddening, many a woman and many a girl who were each raped by at least one fertile man or boy. Having said that, my explicit conviction that Mother Nature is sometimes cruel is, needless to say, given substance by the undeniable fact that there are gazillions of couples who She relentlessly refuses to bless or curse with the child or children that they are each relentlessly praying for and frequently trying to bring into existence.

As I have just attempted to show or remind the reader, Society, like Mother Nature, has a vested interest in the survival of the human race, which, of course, cannot be achieved without perpetual production of children. Having said that, as I have already argued, unlike that of Mother Nature, Society's life is dependent on the existence of human beings, which, of course, means that Society needs us way more than Mother Nature needs us. If Mother Nature really needs us, that is. That is why Society, like Mother Nature, continues to use children to replace adults, especially those who are the nearest to the age to which the oldest person who has ever lived has failed to add yet another year, and, of course, people who are buried or cremated before they reach adulthood. In other words, children are nothing but seeds with which Society and Mother Nature continuously attempt to prevent the extinction of some forest called human beings—creatures without whom, as I have already asserted, Society, unlike Mother Nature, cannot exist.

Secular Natalism

In Her endeavour to prevent the extinction of human beings, Mother Nature—as I have already asserted—uses orgasms and our frequent urge to seek satisfaction of our sexual needs, whereas Society—because She is not that powerful—uses natalism, that is, an attitude or policy that promotes human reproduction.

For this part of our exploration, I will use and exclusively focus on countries, even though those that are secular are, of course, not the only secular entities that encourage many a fertile human being to always or occasionally sleep with at least one fertile human being whose reproductive organs are unlike theirs without the use of any of the many types of contraceptives. Having said that, I will not touch on each and every reason why countries use policies that encourage human reproduction. What's more, not only will some of the things that I am about to assert apply only to twenty-first century countries, there may be one or two modern countries to which those assertions do not apply—but I doubt it.

Before we explore what I believe are the main if not

the only reasons why countries encourage their citizens to procreate, let us touch on some of the tactics with which many a country has enticed and/or coerced, and continues to entice and/or coerce, gazillions of its sane citizens into producing children. It goes without saying that, as those readers who had not realized when they read the very first word of the last sentence should have realized by the time they read the very last word of that sentence, in its never-ending endeavour to dramatically increase the number of its fertile citizens who will each be a parent on their deathday, many a country has used, and many a country uses, a stick (or sticks), a carrot (or carrots), or both; that is to say, a method that is (or methods that are) characterized by the threat of punishment, the offer of reward, or both.

Let us start with the sticks. In its endeavour to increase or at least maintain the number of its native citizens, many a country uses or once used tax. In 1941, for example, the income tax of men between the ages of 20 and 50, and women between the ages of 20 and 45, who were not only citizens of the Soviet Union but also had no or less than three children were increased

by six percent—if they were childless, one percent—
if they had one child, or half a percent—if they had
two children. That tax was, according to many a his-
tory book, eventually called a tax on "bachelors, single and childless citizens of the U.S.S.R."[1] Needless to
say, the sad yet funny thing about taxing the childless is that, as an inevitable result that was desired by
those states, innumerable couples, believe it or not,
have each brought a child or children into this troubled world of ours mainly or only to evade that tax,
even though for most people the annual cost of raising
a single child was, I presume, way more than whatever amount of money that they each had to pay annually because they were childless (or a parent to one
or two children), or would have had to pay annually if
they had remained childless (or a parent to one or two
children).

Let us now touch on one of the carrots. In 2005, in
his endeavour to improve the region's then depressing death-to-birth ratio (a feat that has automatically
contributed, might automatically contribute, or would
have automatically contributed to Russia's then endeavour to fight its birthrate crisis by increasing the

size of its population, which was then declining by at least 700,000 people each year[2]), Sergey Ivanovich Morozov, the then governor of Ulyanovsk Oblast, a federal subject of Russia, declared the twelfth of September a "Day of Conception," which is, as some of us know, also known as "Procreation Day."[3] The goal is, on that holiday, to give couples time off from work so that they can conceive … or at least attempt to. To tell you the truth, I know not whether or not single people, people who are each in a relationship that has at least one infertile partner, and couples that are each made up of individuals who both have a womb or testicles, are each required to set foot in their employer's yard before the end of that day. But that is neither here nor there. To this part of our exploration, that is.

Make no mistake, the twelfth of September is not a randomly selected date. That day, that is, the Day of Conception, is exactly "nine months" before Russia Day, that is, the twelfth of June, which obviously means that, in addition to growing or maintaining the size of Russia's population, the goal is to have as many females-who-will-have-managed-to-fall-pregnant as possible to each "give birth to a patriot or patriots" on

Russia Day. Couples who give birth on Russia Day are each guaranteed, by the regional government, one of a variety of prizes such as cash, refrigerators, television sets, and washing machines. What's more, every single year one lucky couple that gives birth on Russia Day will be picked to win the grand prize: a brand-new Russian-made SUV called the UAZ Patriot.[4] (By the way, I used to be against parents keeping such secrets from their children, until I learned about Russia's Day of Conception and the carrots that its officials use or once used. I mean, I do not know about the reader, but I would rather not know the reason or any of the reasons why my parents have decided to bring me into existence than find out that one of the reasons or the only reason why they have brought me into this troubled world of ours is because they wanted to stand a chance of winning an SUV, a washing machine, or a television set.)

Needless to say, that is the how. Let us now, before we explore the why, put countries—and the human beings they cage—under the microscope.

I am of the unshakable belief that, if truth be told, countries are selfish, which is inevitable because

countries are made up of and are, I believe, led by selfish individuals. And that, as far as I can see, is by no
means a fallacy of composition, that is, the error that
arises when one infers that something is true of the
whole from the fact that it is true of some *part* of the
whole (or even of *every* proper part).[5] As I have made
known in "The Selfish Genie," an essay with which I
have attempted to substantiate my unshakable belief
that all human beings are selfish and that it is humanly impossible to be selfless, by *selfish* I do not mean
"lacking consideration for others," I mean "concerned
chiefly with one's own personal profit or pleasure."
Obviously, "others," when it comes to countries, refers to other countries. It goes without saying that in
the nature of things the invention of countries, as I
have lamented in *Divided & Conquered*, has divided
inhabitants of most if not all continents into citizens
and foreigners. And, as if that were not enough, the
institution of the family (by means of the very same
things, namely, walls and fences) divides citizens, say,
South Africans, into the Joneses, the Coetzees, the
Naidoos, the Mokhonoanas, et cetera, et cetera.

Anyway, as might have been expected, countries,

like their citizens, secretly use each other as nothing but a means to an end, a selfish end.

I am, in addition to that, of the unshakable belief that most if not all sane human beings each belong to either of the following two groups: (1) powerless people who, one, are impressed by and/or envious of powerful people, and, two, are consciously or unconsciously craving power; and, of course, (2) powerful people who are each preoccupied with their desire to at least maintain their power if they fail to become more powerful or, if possible, the most powerful.

In the previous sentence, I, with the word *power*, mean "the capacity or ability to direct or influence the behaviour of others or the course of events."[6] For the most part, that capacity or ability comes, when it comes to human beings, in the form of wealth and/or fame, which—in addition to using it to make as much money as they possibly can and/or to influence innumerable sane human beings to whom they are not strangers—most sane human beings who have managed to attain and retain fame each uses it to dramatically increase their name's chances of being remembered until Jesus comes back, since their heart cannot do what they consciously or unconsciously lust for, that is to say, for it to beat until Jesus returns. When it comes to countries, however, that capacity or ability usually comes in the form of (1) *colonialism*, i.e., the conquering and ruling of one country by another, with a large migration of the oppressing country's people to the newly conquered country, or (2) *imperialism*, i.e., the expansion of a country's sphere of control, without the necessity of settlement.[7]

Indeed, most if not all countries, like pretty much all of their sane citizens, are greedy. By *greedy* I mean that not only do they have an intense and selfish desire for things such as wealth, possessions, and power, they wish to possess way more than they need or deserve. Greed is, according to Erich Fromm, the natural outcome of the having orientation (that is to say, if having is the basis of one's sense of identity because one is of the belief that we are what we have), which, thanks to the wish to have, inevitably leads to the desire to have much, to have more, to have most.[8] Greed is, according to Mokokoma Mokhonoana, a contagious mental illness without which civilization as we know it would not have been possible. Unlike Mignon

McLaughlin, who remarked that "we are all born brave, trusting and greedy, and most of us manage to remain greedy," I do not believe that we are born greedy. Having said that, as the reader is likely to have gathered from what I have just said about civilization, I agree with what would be left of the following statement, which is said to have been said or written by McLaughlin, if we were to edit the first three words out, "Be glad that you're greedy; the national economy would collapse if you weren't."

Milton Friedman, an American economist who received the 1976 Nobel Memorial Prize in Economic Sciences, was once asked the following relevant question by an interviewer, "When you see around the globe the maldistribution of wealth, the desperate plight of millions of people in underdeveloped countries; when you see so few haves and so many have-nots; when you see the greed and the concentration of power; did you ever have a moment of doubt about capitalism, and whether greed is a good idea to run on?" And he, among other things, said "Well, first of all ... tell me, is there some society you know that doesn't run on greed? You think Russia doesn't run on greed? You think China doesn't run on greed? *What is greed?* Of course, none of us are greedy; it's only the other fellow who's greedy. The world runs on individuals pursuing their separate interests."

Anyway, as an inevitable result, most if not all countries, with the exception of the most powerful country, each strives to be the most powerful country. The most powerful country strives to remain the most powerful country, which, when occupying that coveted spot, a country usually achieves by getting more and more powerful, whereas—in addition to striving to be the most powerful country—most of the remaining countries each strives to at least be one of the most powerful countries. With the exception of the most powerful country, the most powerful countries each strives to remain one of the most powerful countries while they each move heaven and earth to increase their chances of being the most powerful country, whereas—in addition to being the most powerful country or at least one of the most powerful countries—the least powerful countries each strives to at least vacate the group that is made up of the least powerful countries (as we all know, many a poor man who has a lust for riches finds comfort in the fact that he is certainly not the poorest and/or that he could have definitely been poorer; the same can, needless to say, be said about, say, an ugly woman who has a lust for one of the membership cards that are given to no one but members of Beautiful Women's Club, and a fat man who has a lust for the kind of physique that stands a chance of being used to sell underwear by companies such as Calvin Klein Inc.).

Indeed, I am of the unshakable belief that, if truth be told, countries are cannibalistic; they, without a doubt, do not have to be, but, sad to say, they are. Given the chance, most if not all countries—with, of course, the exception of the least powerful country—will each devour or at least attempt to devour at least one country that is weaker or less powerful than it is. And if it were then possible for man to literally take a country that is not located next to his and then add it to his in order to make his physically bigger, the part of planet earth on which one finds the piece of land we call Africa would today be part of the Atlantic and the Indian Ocean. What's more, if the mania for dominance that most if not all countries suffer from continued, and it were still possible for us to literally take a country that is not located next to ours and then add it to ours to make ours physically bigger, planet earth would have ended up or would eventually end up as a single country, and, because countries are cursed with an insatiable desire to have way more than they have, we would, after that, eventually start looking for ways to "colonize" or "imperialize" other planets. Obviously, that will seem far-fetched to readers who either do not know or have forgotten that many a European country has for a very long time blatantly chewed pretty much every single part of Africa.

The primary if not the only reason why many a country did not colonize another country or other countries is, I believe, because it was still growing or at least attempting to grow into a country whose size or power would have then made it possible or easier for it to colonize another country or other countries. In other words, most if not all countries that have never had a colony would have each colonized another country or other countries, or they would have at least attempted to do that, if they had "needed" to do that, or, as is probably the case in many a case, if they could do that. (Obviously, it is impossible for all countries to be colonizers *at the very same time*.) As we all know, one, many a survivor of a plane crash who is or was against cannibalism and had never eaten human flesh once found themselves in a situation where they had to either eat human flesh, or go the way of all flesh, and, two, many if not most slaves would have each readily jumped, and many if not most slaves would each readily jump, at the opportunity to be a master, if such an opportunity presents or had presented itself.

Here is yet another way of saying one of the things that I have just said: Just like how most if not all poor boys look up to and aspire to someday be rich men, most if not all underdeveloped and developing countries look up to and aspire to someday be developed countries. It goes without saying that the realization of the latter's aspiration will come at a price, namely, harmful effects on planet earth and the atmosphere. As Mario Molina, a Nobel Prize-winning chemist, is said to have said in an interview, "If we look at the world's population, maybe about a fourth of those are in the rich countries responsible for most of the pollution. The other three-fourths have a right to vigorous economic development, to high standards of living. But the planet is just too small for these developing countries to repeat the economic growth in the same way that the rich countries have done it in the past. We don't have enough natural resources, we don't have enough atmosphere."[9]

Anyway, I do not think that any of the many countries that have each bitten off and then unashamedly chewed a piece or pieces of the pie called Africa did so because it was starving. If that is not the reason why some countries have colonized some countries, which I doubt it is, then one can, because countries are run by human beings, use that to substantiate my conviction that pretty much all sane human beings are greedy; that is to say, we, with the exception of a relatively small number of people, have an intense and selfish desire to have way more than we need. Needless to say, the average sane human being would have already seen the average modern country's true colours and those of the average sane human being, which— as I have already asserted—are like two peas in a pod, if there were no laws. As a matter of fact, most of the people who are each regarded as a good person would not be regarded as good people, if they were not terrified of the penalties that are sometimes inflicted on some sane human beings who, after breaking the law, get caught ... by police officers who, needless to say, cannot be bought.

I strongly believe that, if truth be told, the number of men who have each slept with a female without her permission would have probably increased at least a millionfold, if there were no laws against that deed, and many if not most females would have never heard, from a man's mouth, the phrase "I'd like to get to know you better," which, in many if not most cases, is, of course, a euphemism for "I want to fuck you." To be sure, there exists many a man who, from a woman who he has just impressed or is trying to impress, wants to get into her heart way more than he wants to get into her pants. Having said that, in many if not most cases, all that a sane man wants when he tries to impress a woman or women is a vagina or vaginas with which he, every now and then, will, with the woman or women's permission, temporarily get rid of the recurrent urge to seek satisfaction of his sexual needs. I mean, whenever he does, why—instead of asking her to be his friend—does the average heterosexual man beg a woman he likes or pretends to like to be his girl-friend, if he does not have the desire to sleep with her then or someday? In other words, to ask a man whether or not he has a girlfriend is to talk about his sex life. If you disagree with that, then how in the name of God do you differentiate between a man's girlfriend and a girl that is a friend to the man?

What's more, most if not all modern countries would not be or seem civil like they are *forced* to be or to seem by the so-called international law, if there were no laws, and many a country would without a doubt still be colonized by a country that is more powerful than it is. "Since Hobbes, one has seen in power the basic motive of human behaviour." Erich Fromm is said to have written. "The following centuries, however, gave increased weight to legal and moral factors which tended to curb power."[10] As might have been expected, that has left many a human being with the belief that countries like each other, which is definitely not true; like it is not true when it comes to human beings: the last time everyone loved or at least liked everyone was when the world had a population of about 4.

Obviously, such laws do not (try to) protect only weak or less powerful countries that would have each become or continued being a victim of colonization if those laws did not exist; some of them (try to) protect weak or less powerful citizens who, if it were not for the law, would have definitely been abused by pretty much all of the citizens who are powerful unlike them or more powerful than them. Indeed, when it comes to our never-ending endeavour to end or at least minimize human violence, laws that regulate or at least attempt to regulate the actions of countries are as necessary as those that regulate or at least attempt to regulate the actions of citizens. As we all know, as if forever exploiting or attempting to exploit each other were not enough, a group of sane human beings who have just reached the end of a war against a common enemy of theirs will sooner or later start or continue killing and/or fighting against each other.

I have two questions for readers to whom I have come across as a misanthrope: Would we have come up with laws against the act of taking someone's property without permission or legal right and without intending to return it, the act of having sexual inter-course with someone without their permission, and the act of ending the life of another human being without permission from the powers that be, if human beings were not already doing or capable of doing and likely to do that? And would we have come up with the so-called international law, if countries were not already doing or capable of doing and likely to do whatever it is that international law attempts to prevent or minimize?

Finally, because I have disillusioned or at least attempted to disillusion many a reader who desperately needed or needs to be disillusioned with regard to the humaneness of the average modern country and that of the average sane human being, let us now explore the primary if not the only reasons why countries promote human reproduction.

The most obvious and most important reason why a country encourages human reproduction is because its survival is dependent on its having human beings caged within its own borders. In other words, the primary goal of each and every country, like that of most if not all organisms, is to evade its own death (as many times as it possibly can). By that I, of course, refer to a state where a "country" no longer has human inhabitants, and the ensuing collapse of its economy, which is without a doubt innumerable millions of times less unlikely than the former. Needless to say, the economy of a country needs a very large proportion of its population to be economically active (that is to say, each and every one of those people has to sell their time, energy, skills, and/or knowledge, and, if need be, their souls) for that country, with the desperately needed help of its inhabitants who are economically active, to be able to take care of its young dependents and retirees, people from whom it cannot make money through income tax because they are not working yet or anymore. To the aforementioned people one can, of course, add the many millions of sane human beings who do not work even though they definitely have the desire, the time, and—in countless cases— the skills to work, and they are neither too young nor too old to work.

If it fails to change that, a country whose death rate is higher than its birth rate will eventually be blessed or cursed with depopulation, which, as we all know, inevitably changes or even inverts the ideal population pyramid, which has young dependents at the very bottom, economically active people in the middle, and elderly dependents at the very top. When a population pyramid of an industrialized country is turned upside down, the number of its retirees who its economically active inhabitants have to support financially increases dramatically, whereas—perhaps more threatening to the well-being of the country's economy—the number of its young dependents who are and those who are going to be groomed to replace the aging workforce decreases dramatically.

Speaking of depopulation, it is, I believe, worth reminding the reader that while most if not all definitions of *overpopulation* mention or at least allude to carrying capacity (that is to say, the maximum number of individuals that an area's resources can sustain indefinitely), *underpopulation* is usually defined as a state in which a country's population has declined so much that it cannot support its current economic system, which, of course, then means that, contrary to popular belief, the two terms are not antonyms—the latter is, as far as I can see, strictly an economic term and concept. What's more, it is worth noting that in at least one case the irony was that depopulation, which then shrunk the country's economy, was caused by war, which was started by the unprovoked country in its relentless endeavour to grow its own economy. Obviously, in many such a case, only the economy of the country that warred only to defend itself was shrunk.

Now that that is out of the way, let us focus on most if not all countries' secondary goal, which, I strongly believe, is the same as most sane human beings' secondary goal, namely, to obtain or increase or at least retain power, which, in addition to wealth, usually comes in the form of fame, when it comes to human beings, and military destructiveness, when it comes to countries. It goes without saying that more often than not when we call a country powerful that country is so deemed because it is wealthy. Granted, a country can be called powerful because of nothing but the destructiveness of its military, but—like they literally do whenever they are used—weapons of mass destruction cost an arm and a leg.

Wealth is, I believe, more important and more empowering than military might because, needless to say, money makes it possible for a small group of people or even a single person to control the thoughts and the actions of millions of sane people without the use of force or threats—as we all know, among other possibilities, money was invented to make it possible for a foolish man to control wise men; a weak man, strong men; a child, old men; an ignorant man, knowledgeable men; and for a dwarf to control giants. Because of that, country A can easily give some of its taxpayers' money to country B so that it, country B, will allow it, country A, to "borrow" some or all members of country B's armed forces in order to increase country A's chances of defeating country C, a country that it is warring or about to war against. On top of that, because of the enormous importance that most sane human beings have attached to money, which—in the nature of things—has given money power over most sane human beings, country A can pay some members of country C's armed forces and/or some of its civilians to help it in its endeavour to win the war against country C, their very own native country. (Speaking of armed forces, their existence, like some of the things that I have asserted earlier, gives substance to my unshakable belief that we sane human beings are not as humane as or humane like we are made to seem by our fear of the penalties that are sometimes inflicted on some sane human beings who, after breaking the law, get caught ... by police officers who, as I have effortlessly rhymed earlier, cannot be bought. I mean, armed forces are definitely not meant to protect us from attacks by Mother Nature; they are each meant to protect their own country from attacks by other countries, not from the so-called acts of God.)

For this part of our exploration, I will, because of that, focus only on most if not all countries' lust for and relentless pursuit of wealth—money, to be precise. Not only will doing that minimize the number of unnecessary sentences herein, and not only can money buy one valuable possessions whose abundance (like the abundance of money) we call wealth, money buys every country people (armed forces, to be exact) with whom it protects its own wealth and its own citizens, particularly those who it is using in its never-ending endeavour to become wealthy or wealthier or to at least remain wealthy. What's more, I will, in order to save my ink and the reader's time, focus only on tax (income tax and valued-added tax, to be precise) instead of touching on every single thing with which countries make money, which, of course, means that I am by no means ignorant of the fact that there are other kinds of taxes (such as property tax) and other things (such as state-owned companies) with which countries make money.

Let us get the most obvious out of the way. One, most if not all countries derive a significant proportion of their revenues from taxation, and, two, they impose tax on (some) organizations and (some) individuals, as workers (through income tax) and/or as consumers (through valued-added tax and the like). Needless to say, that means that one of the reasons why a country encourages its citizens to reproduce is because it desperately wants to avoid not having enough employers, employees, and consumers to keep its economy healthy or at least not dead. Although they are without a doubt also consumers, to the aforementioned people one can, of course, add many millions of people who are unemployed, seeing that most if not all companies benefit immensely from the mere existence of many if not most skilled but unemployed people, because they make many if not most of the companies' employees a hundred times more replaceable and, in the nature of things, a thousand times less likely to demand to be paid, say, twice as much as they are currently earning, even if they deserve to be paid at least thrice as much as they currently earn. That means more money for the companies. And more money for them means more money for countries, seeing that, needless to say, the incomes they tax (the companies', their shareholders', their CEOs', etc.) are way more than they would have been if those employees were paid more. Granted, countries would still receive a portion of the extra money via income tax if it were paid to underpaid employees instead of being pocketed by their employers, but chances are that the countries would receive way less money than they do via income tax, because not a few hundred thousands if not millions of employees who earn less than they deserve earn so little that their incomes would still be too little for the countries to tax, even if they were to be doubled ... or even tripled.

There is, of course, another way in which countries, especially industrialized ones, benefit immensely from unemployment: the cruelty of unemployment has left most if not all underpaid employees with the unshakable belief that being underpaid is better than being unemployed; and a very large number of those employees strongly believe that cheap labour is also better than unemployment. It goes without saying that those beliefs each plays or used to play an important role in most if not all countries' relentless endeavours to make as much money as they possibly can make each and every year, especially the latter (cheap labour has played and probably still plays an extremely important role in the growth of China's economy, which is currently the envy of pretty much all countries).

Anyway, in their never-ending endeavours to become wealthy or wealthier or to at least remain wealthy, countries, in a nutshell, desperately need, among other things, workers. But not nearly as much as they need companies. To start with, it would still be possible for many a country to make a lot of money through income tax if only a tiny fraction of the people who live within its borders had jobs, and not a single one of its inhabitants purchased any of the products that are produced and/or sold (or any of the services that are provided) within its borders. Granted, those countries would still need a very large number of people who will continuously purchase some of those products and some of those services in order for the countries to make a lot of money from the taxation of the revenues of the companies that are or would be producing and/or selling those products and/or providing those services within their borders, but, in each and every case, those consumers, needless to say, need not live within the country's borders. Secondly, many if not most workers, as we all know, can each be easily replaced, or rather superseded, by a machine, which— unlike or compared to a human worker—need not be paid, does not want or even need to occasionally take a leave of absence, makes fewer or no mistakes, never strikes to decrease its chances of not being blessed or cursed with a salary increase, does not take lunch and/ or smoke breaks, works with the very same amount of energy and the very same amount of enthusiasm throughout the day (even on weekends, holidays, and nonpaydays), et cetera, et cetera. (Perhaps the reason why most jobs that can be easily performed by machines are not and will probably never be performed by machines is because—seeing that they are not and will probably never be paid at all, and since they do not need or even want the things that we need and those that we want—machines cannot replace human beings as consumers, creatures that are as important to the health, nay life, of the economy as producers are.) And, thirdly, although many if not most companies would still be able to produce the products and/ or to provide the services that they are currently producing and/or providing if they got rid of most if not all of their human workers, only a tiny fraction of the people who are employed to produce products and/ or to provide services would still be able to do that if their employers were to stop providing them with the facilities and/or the resources that enable them to do their work.

As might have been expected, pretty much every single country—government, to be precise—tries to please the hundreds of big companies that operate within its borders way more than it tries to please the many millions of individuals who live within the very same borders (with, of course, the exception of a relatively small number of individuals who have wealth, which, in pretty much all cases, came from a big company that is or was partially or entirely owned by them, their family, or their family member or members). It goes without saying that that would not necessarily be a bad thing if most companies did not deem and, as an inevitable result, treat the environment and/or pretty much all human beings as if it and/or they were secondary to profit. (Those who profit the most from such companies can, of course, argue, with reason, that in reality most human beings are not, to most human beings, more important than money.) "Surely by now there can be few here who still believe the purpose of government is to protect us from the destructive activities of corporations." Derrick Jensen is said to have written in *Endgame, Vol. 1: The Problem of Civilization*. "At last most of us must understand that the opposite is true: that the primary purpose of government is to protect those who run the economy from the outrage of injured citizens."

There is, of course, another similarity between most if not all countries and most sane adults that is worth touching on: they all use nothing but the amount of money that they have each made in a year as an index of growth. Most sane adults use their remuneration, which in most cases comes in the form of wages or a salary, whereas countries use their GNP (i.e., gross national product, the total value of all services provided and all goods produced within the borders of a country during one year *plus* "the income earned by [its] residents from overseas investments *minus* income earned within [its] economy by overseas residents"), whose growth does not, as the reader is about to be reminded, necessarily mean that the life of the average inhabitant or even that of the average citizen of the country has improved in any way that really matters to them. As we all know, there are millions of people whose lives have remained more or less the same and millions of people whose lives have actually gotten worse during the very same year during which their country's economy has grown exponentially. Perhaps one of the causes of those common occurrences is many a maneuver by a relatively small number of rich people who have realized that, as I have asserted elsewhere through an aphorism of mine, it is in the best interest of the rich to preserve poverty.

"But even if we act to erase material poverty, there is another greater task, it is to confront the poverty of satisfaction—purpose and dignity—that afflicts us all." Robert F. Kennedy is said to have said at the University of Kansas on the eighteenth of March 1968. "Too much and for too long, we seemed to have surrendered personal excellence and community values in the mere accumulation of material things. Our gross national product, now, is over 800 billion dollars a year, but that gross national product—if we judge the United States of America by that—that gross national product counts air pollution and cigarette advertising, and ambulances to clear our highways of carnage. It counts special locks for our doors and the jails for the people who break them. It counts the destruction of the redwood and the loss of our natural wonder in chaotic sprawl. It counts napalm and counts nuclear warheads and armored cars for the police to fight the riots in our cities. It counts Whitman's rifle and Speck's knife, and the television programs which glorify violence in order to sell toys to our children. Yet the gross national product does not allow for the health of our children, the quality of their education or the joy of their play. It does not include the beauty of our poetry or the strength of our marriages, the intelligence of our public debate or the integrity of our public officials. It measures neither our wit nor our courage, neither our wisdom nor our learning, neither our compassion nor our devotion to our country; it measures everything in short, except that which makes life worthwhile."[11]

Obviously, measuring most of the things that make life worthwhile to most sane human beings is by no means nearly as easy as measuring things such as GDP and GNP. Having said that, as Herman E. Daly and Joshua Farley are said to have written in *Ecological Economics: Principles and Applications*, "Even if we can never quantify [satisfaction or happiness]... as precisely as we currently quantify GNP,... perhaps it is better to be vaguely right than precisely wrong."[12]

Before we conclude this part of our exploration, allow me to share yet another reason, which countries almost never mention, why each and every country moves mountains to get its citizens to reproduce: In a word, to keep the number of its legal and illegal immigrants forever disproportionate to the number of its citizens whose ancestors' forefathers were born within its own borders. (I mean, what would, say, USA, be, and how much USA would USA be, if most of its citizens were born in, say, Mexico, Afghanistan, India, Zimbabwe, and China?). And that is, of course, regarded as a patriotic thing to do, which, by the way, is why I am of the unshakable belief that patriotism is the narcissism of countries.

To sum up, in addition to things such as preventing itself from becoming a piece of land that is inhabited by less than one human being, each and every country relentlessly strives to become wealthy or wealthier or to at least remain wealthy. And that, needless to say, necessitates human beings, as producers and as consumers, and, as an inevitable result, human reproduction, because human beings are not immortal. What's more, for their never-ending endeavours to obtain or retain wealth, countries desperately need companies, because they—unlike most human beings—have the means of production, and human beings, because they—unlike all companies—have the means of reproduction.

Religious Natalism

In addition to the reasons that I have already touched on, some of the most common reasons why many a sane human being reproduces intentionally are: (1) they have the ability to—with the help of at least one fertile member of the sex that is opposite to theirs—produce children, and they strongly believe that they were endowed with that for a reason, namely, to produce children; (2) most sane human beings have either reproduced or attempted to reproduce, are attempting to reproduce, or would love to reproduce someday; and/or (3) they are of the unshakable belief that God has definitely commanded the human race, or rather human beings who He did not curse or bless with infertility, to reproduce.

I am, of course, referring to Genesis 1:28 ("Then God blessed them and said, 'Be fruitful and multiply. Fill the earth and govern it. Reign over the fish in the sea, the birds in the sky, and all the animals that scurry along the ground.'"), which is believed by many if not most believers to be the very first and thus the most important command that God gave to human beings. In the nature of things, most if not all of those people—who form a very big if not the biggest portion of the human race, regard human reproduction as an obligation and, as an inevitable result, not reproducing as disobedience to God. In other words, one of the reasons—in some cases, the only reason—why some people reproduce is because they desperately want to be or remain in God's good books, because they strongly believe that that feat will dramatically increase their chances of going to heaven, which, we are told, will give them what the average sane human being desperately craves, namely, immortality. (It goes without saying that even those of us who are going to hell will get eternal life—if that territory really exists outside religious books and the minds of believers, that is. Having said that, given the choice, instead of being grilled until hell freezes over, the average sane human being would, needless to say, rather spend forever idling in an extremely fertile garden, next to a lamb or a chicken or a parrot, which they do not secretly want to eat, and a lion or a tiger or a crocodile, which does not secretly want to eat them.)

Naturally, that verse is one of the things that are

sometimes questioned and/or attacked by many if not most of the people who advocate the protection of the environment, people to whom life after death is either not important at all, or not as important as life before death. Although I do not know without a shadow of a doubt, I do not believe that most of the people who have criticized that verse did so because they are opposed to human reproduction. I believe that what many if not most of them have a problem with is that that verse says absolutely nothing about the number of children that fertile believers each ought to strive to bring into this troubled world of ours, which, as we all know, probably each and every believer believes is the one and only doorway to both heaven and hell.

Like the consumption of pork, the act or the state of being in love or in bed with someone whose genitals are the same as yours, and the use of one's own finger or hand instead of a vagina or a penis in one's endeavour to bring about an orgasm, because it was written in a language and then translated into languages whose words and sentences are in many a case open to more than one interpretation, and because it is divided into the Old Testament and the New Testament, the Bible has divided not a few millions of literate human beings, many if not most of whom are Christians, with regard to what some verses mean and, as a result, what God wants and what He does not want: (1) some people strongly believe that "be fruitful and multiply" is "the most tragic translation error"; (2) although they and, as far as I can tell, such verses do not mention the number of children that one has to have before one is said to have many children, some people strongly believe that having many children is a blessing from God; (3) because of verses such as John 15:8, "You give glory to my Father when you produce a lot of fruit and therefore show that you are my disciples," some people strongly believe that having many children is a way of giving God glory; (4) some people strongly believe that "Christianity doesn't promote procreation. It did in Old Testament times, but now God gives us the choice of whether or not to reproduce"[13]; (5) because they strongly believe that having many children is a blessing, and that only God is allowed to decide on the number of children that one will have parented come one's deathday, some people strongly believe that people who are fertile ought to strive to produce

83

as many children as they possibly can; (6) because they strongly believe that God is the only being who is allowed to decide on the number of children who one will have brought into this troubled world of ours come the day on which one is going to exit the land of the living, that it is unbiblical to limit the number of children to whom one is a parent, some believers are strongly against family planning: "People who are afraid to give up control of their family size to the Lord are, according to [the authors of *A Full Quiver*, Rick and Jan Hess, an American evangelical couple], showing a lack of faith." Reverend J. Moesker is said to have written in one of his articles. "[The Hesses] state in chapter 7 of their book, 'We know couples who have read this book or with whom we've discussed these issues and they have no arguments or questions. They simply do not trust God. They may opt to be moderately fruitful and add instead of multiply. They choose to fill perhaps one or two bedrooms of their home rather than the world.'"14; and (7) as might have been expected, some people strongly believe that fertile people who use contraceptives are each preventing God from giving them a blessing or blessings in the form of a child, another child, more children, many children, or, preferably, as many children as they can possibly produce; in other words, to some believers, being on the pill or using a condom is a nonverbal way of telling God to go to hell.

It goes without saying that another reason why some believers reproduce is because they not only believe that children are a gift from God but also derive great pleasure from receiving gifts, and that to that widespread belief one can attribute verses such as Psalm 127:3, which asserts that "Children are a gift from the Lord; they are a reward from him." Needless to say, if children are really a gift from God, then one can, with reason, presume that: (1) God does not hate premarital sex like or as much as many a believer believes that He does, seeing that He has given and He continues to give the gift of a child or children to many an unmarried person; what's more, He has refused and He continues to refuse to give many a married couple the gift of children or even a single child—a breathing gift that they have relentlessly begged for, and they continue to relentlessly beg for, through a nonverbal prayer called unprotected sex; and (2) God does not hate nonbelievers like or as much as many a believer believes that He does, seeing that there are many millions of fertile nonbelievers and many millions of infertile believers; on top of that, hundreds of thousands if not millions of believers have each made a child or children with a nonbeliever ... or nonbelievers.

There is, of course, a relevant and commonly asked question that I have not touched on as yet that deserves to be touched on, namely, Is God's command in question, that is to say, "be fruitful and multiply," aimed at fertile believers—or is it aimed at fertile human beings? If truth be told, I have absolutely no idea. But I know without a shadow of a doubt that countless people strongly believe that that command is aimed at fertile human beings, whereas innumerable believers strongly believe that it is aimed only at fertile believers—and that is probably because, according to some people, the Bible has divided children into two categories: "Scripture draws a fundamental distinction between the children of the righteous (of whom there are never enough)," Mary Pride is said to have asserted, "and the children of the wicked (of whom there are always too many)."[15]

Having said that, there are, of course, believers who did not reproduce by mistake or mainly to please God. Anyway, when it comes to their being or their intention to someday be parents, the primary goals of many if not most of the believers who do not fall under that category of believers can, in descending order of importance, be summed up as follows: (1) to obey and thus please God; (2) to prevent the extinction of human beings; (3) to prevent the extinction of believers; and (4) to increase believers' chances of not being outnumbered by nonbelievers—but, whether or not they have any, some, or even all of the aforementioned goals, most if not all believers are, needless to say, secretly or even openly praying for and/or working extremely hard to bring about the extinction of nonbelievers.

Indeed, what I have asserted with regard to the apparent unity of citizens of any country—that they are divided by at least one thing as soon as they are no longer united by a common enemy of theirs (e.g., an epidemic or citizens of another country or other countries), can definitely be said about believers, because believers are united only when they are around nonbelievers and when they are talking about them or atheism, and whenever they are not doing that and there are no nonbelievers or at least one nonbeliever around to be used as cement by believers, pretty much all Christians, Jews, Muslims, et cetera, resuscitate and then occasionally nourish their "us and them" attitude; that is to say, they each return to and then preserve their secretly seeing each and every believer who does not belong to their religion as a competitor and/or a threat to their own religion. Without a doubt, the very same thing can be said about the apparent unity of Christians, because many millions of people who are occasionally united by Christianity are every now and then divided by Christian denominations such as Catholicism and Protestantism. What's more, those who are sometimes united by Protestantism are from time to time divided by Protestant denominations such as Lutheranism, Methodism, Calvinism, Anglicanism, and Pentecostalism.

In other words, among other reasons, innumerable Christians, Jews, Muslims, etc., reproduce in order to help members of their own religion to attempt to outnumber or prevent being outnumbered by members of other religions. In addition to other objectives, for example, such Christians reproduce in order to keep Christianity the world's biggest organized religion, whereas such Muslims reproduce as an attempt to help Islam to occupy the coveted spot that is currently occupied by Christianity. And that is not where the competition ends. Once one sees through the apparent unity of Christians, one will realize that one of the reasons why some Anglicans reproduce is because they want to outnumber or prevent being outnumbered by Lutherans, Methodists, Pentecostals, et cetera.

It goes without saying that a believer can increase the number of believers by convincing a nonbeliever to believe in God, that a Christian can increase the number of Christians by convincing a non-Christian to believe in Jesus Christ and his teachings, and that a Lutheran can increase the number of Lutherans by persuading a non-Lutheran to join the Lutheran Church, instead of making a child who the believer, Christian, or Lutheran will patiently mold into a believer, a Christian, or a Lutheran. Indeed, there are reasons why, for example, many a believer attempts, has attempted, or will attempt to increase the number of believers by having unprotected sexual intercourse instead of a protracted discourse. Here are some of them: (1) it is way easier to gradually mold your own baby into, say, a Muslim or a Methodist, than it is to persuade an adult or even a teenager to adhere to Islam or to join the Methodist Church, even if they are already a believer; (2) the average adult has had sex innumerable times more than they have formed an opinion of their own; (3) inducing an orgasm is usually way more pleasurable than coming up with a plausible reason, or parroting one or some of the assertions or beliefs that the average believer regards as plausible reasons, why nonbelievers ought to believe in God; and (4) a single instance of unprotected sexual intercourse can lead to a believer's accomplishment of multiple goals of theirs (such as to comply with what they believe God has commanded fertile human beings or fertile believers to do, to prevent the extinction of believers, and to dramatically decrease nonbelievers' chances of outnumbering believers), even if the man ejaculates after only a few seconds.

The Use of Girls by Men

With this part of our exploration I would like to touch on the use of female children that is brought about by the *virgin cleansing myth* (which is, needless to say, also called the *virgin rape myth* or *virgin cure myth*), that is to say, the belief that a man can, by simply having unprotected sex with a female who had never had sex, cure himself of HIV/AIDS or other sexually transmitted diseases. As far as I can see, most if not all of the people who really believe that can be divided into two subgroups: one, those who believe that any female virgin will get the job done, and, two, those who believe that the female virgin needs to be young, very young—an adolescent, a prepubescent, a toddler, or even an infant.

The following are, I believe, some of the reasons why many a man who has raped at least one female as an attempt of his to cure himself of at least one sexually transmitted disease has chosen a female who was then not yet an adult, an adolescent, a prepubescent, or even a toddler: (1) the average six-year-old is more likely to be a virgin than the average twenty-six-year-old; (2) it is way easier to carry or to lure the average six-year-old into a place where they could be secretly raped than it is to do the same thing to the average sixteen-year-old; (3) the average sixteen-year-old victim of unreported rape is a trillion times more likely to eventually report that and/or to reveal the identity of the person who has raped them than most if not all sixteen-month-old victims of rape; and (4) some of the rapists in question believe or believed: one, that a "pure heart" has healing properties; two, that most children's hearts are pure; and, in the nature of things, three, that the younger their victim, the more likely to be pure-hearted they are.

In closing, there are people who, like yours truly, strongly believe that the virgin cleansing myth has increased the number of rape victims who are disabled. Like some of the people who believe that, to the aforementioned increase I attribute the presumption that disabled people are sexually inactive and therefore virgins. It goes without saying that that presumption is erroneous. As some of us know, innumerable disabled people are sexually active, which obviously means that some disabilities do not make sexual intercourse impossible or very difficult. What's more, many a person had sex many a time before they became disabled.

The Use of Children by Companies

Children as Producers

It is a well-known fact that children were for a very long time used as workers by some of the people who benefit or used to benefit from mining, and that tens of thousands of children are found in small-scale gold mines of South America, Asia, and Africa today[16]. Having said that, I will not, with this part of our exploration, focus on that. I am going to focus on the use of children as workers by another industry. But before I do, I would like to share the caption of a cartoon that I was fortunate to come across while I was writing this part of our exploration to which it is relevant: *"Coal Mines – it's why God invented children."*

For this part of our exploration, I would like to touch on the use of children as workers by the chocolate industry. There is a reason why I have decided to focus only on one industry: I am of the unshakable belief that I need not focus on more than one industry in order to stand a chance of achieving what I am about to attempt to achieve with this part of our exploration. What's more, there are a few reasons why I have decided to focus on the chocolate instead of the mining industry. Here are the two most important: (1) until only a few months ago, I, believe it or not, was ignorant of the use of children by cocoa farmers, and, in the nature of things, that has left me with an unshakable belief that, although they probably know that some children were used and some children are used as miners, most adults are ignorant of the chocolate industry's use of minors; and (2) I strongly believe that it is way more difficult for the reader to do something about the use of children by or in some mines than it is for the reader to do something about the use of children by many if not most cocoa farmers.

Cocoa beans are, as we all know, the main ingredient of chocolate, which is, of course, sometimes the main ingredient in things such as cereals, candy bars, biscuits, and Easter eggs. To make chocolate, which is mainly made with cocoa butter and cocoa liquor, a chocolate manufacturer, as far as I can see, either buys cocoa beans and then use them to make cocoa butter and cocoa liquor, or it buys them from at least one company that makes cocoa butter and cocoa liquor from cocoa beans, which it buys from one or some of the many farmers around the world who grow cocoa (most of whom are said to be located in West Africa, which apparently grows most of the world's cocoa beans—seventy percent of the "world's cocoa beans come from four West African countries: Ivory Coast, Ghana, Nigeria and Cameroon"[17]). Either way, that chocolate manufacturer, like most if not all chocolate manufacturers, desperately needs at least one cocoa farmer.

To be sure, in most if not all of the cases where children are illegally used by the industry in question the culprit is the cocoa farmer not the chocolate company. Having said that, pretty much everyone whose protest against the use of children by the chocolate industry I have come across, like yours truly, believes that chocolate companies that use some of the cocoa beans that were bought from cocoa farmers who illegally use children as workers, which is probably to say most if not all of the biggest chocolate companies, are as evil as those farmers.

Contrary to the impression that the previous sentence will leave many a reader with, I am not against all of those chocolate manufacturers. I know that, as buyers, companies, like individuals, can easily support criminals unintentionally or even unknowingly; that, as buyers, we, like companies, can easily be deceived by a seller; which is why I strongly believe that, if truth be told, there is nothing morally wrong with buying stolen goods, unless you know that they were stolen.

Make no mistake, the average cocoa farmer, unlike the average chocolate manufacturer, does not make a lot of money from our consumption of chocolate. (One of the reasons why that is the case is, as far as I can see, because the vast majority of the world's cocoa beans are grown by smallholder farmers, that is, people who each farm on an area of land that is way smaller than a typical farm: "Worldwide, 90% of cocoa is grown on small family farms of 2 to 5 hectares, while just 5% comes from large plantations of 40 hectares or more."[18]. In other words, the number of co-coa farmers is disproportionate to that of chocolate manufacturers.) As a matter of fact, many if not most smallholder cocoa farmers, contrary to what the average person assumes or will in all likelihood assume, do not earn much; they, believe it or not, earn barely enough money to survive.

Indeed, the picture that I am trying to paint would be incomplete if I do not touch on the socio-economic situation that many if not most West African cocoa farmers find themselves in (but to save the reader's precious time, I am going to focus only on Ivory Coast, which is said to be the world's biggest cocoa producer): Those cocoa farmers, like countless countrymen of theirs, live in extreme poverty.

Let us briefly deal with the poverty-stricken cocoa farmers and their poor countrymen separately.

Because of the poverty that surrounds them and their families, innumerable children are forced to work in order for them to contribute to their families' daily endeavours to evade starvation. Some of the children are forced to work by the widespread poverty alone, whereas some are forced to work by not only abject poverty but also their parents. In the nature of things, child trafficking, which is mostly if not only done by people who also do what they do only because they desperately want to evade starvation, is rife in Ivory Coast. Trafficked children, most of whom are said to come from rural areas, are sold to cocoa farmers.[19]

Allow me to tell the reader about some parts of and to cite a few extracts from *The Dark Side of Chocolate*, a documentary that "reveals shocking and disturbing new evidence that child labour, trafficking, and slavery are continuing in the cocoa industry, *nearly ten years after the cocoa industry pledged to end it* [italics mine]."[20] While the creators of the documentary were talking to and secretly filming the local head of the bus companies in Sikasso, a city in the south of Mali, which is one of the world's poorest countries, a man who had just spotted a girl entering a bus with a female trafficker suddenly turns up and then says, "They got a girl. Let's go." By the time they got to the bus, the woman had disappeared. They then asked the girl, who had just told them that she is 12 years old but is suspected by one of the men to be younger, a few questions after they had taken her out of the bus.

Among other things, she told them that she is from Segou, which the narrator says is a village that is 450 kilometers away from the Sikasso bus station. When asked, "What did the woman tell you to expect in the Ivory Coast?", she quickly replied, "She said I would make money." The rescued girl was then asked if she believed the female trafficker, and she said that she did. She instantly answered in the affirmative when she was asked if she missed her family. That question was immediately followed by the question, "What will your parents say if you come home without money?", and she, with an even more sad face, said that they will be angry with her. She was then asked, "What will your parents say when you come home?", and she stopped looking into the camera or at the man who had asked her that question, and then ashamedly said, "They will say that I didn't earn any money," while she directed her gaze towards her feet.

A few minutes before that part, the aforementioned men are shown arriving at a Sikasso bus station, which is not only the junction for all traffic to the Ivory Coast but also—according to the investigators' source—the place from which child trafficking takes place. Because they wanted to know more about the operation, they went to the local union for the city's bus drivers. And after he was asked, "How is it with the trafficking of children?", Idrissa Kantê, General Secretary of the Driver's Union in Sikasso, asserted that "Trafficking of children has always existed. Always. The children are constantly leaving from the bus station. The children who are going to the Ivory Coast are 12-14 years old. The girls are 11-12."

In the nature of things, the abject poverty that innumerable Ivorians find themselves in, as I have said earlier, has left many a child a worker—and in many if not most cases that comes at the expense of schooling. According to an estimate that is in a report by Tulane University, which analyzed data collected during the 2013-2014 harvest season, the number of Ivorian children who were not only between the ages of 5 and 17 at that time but also employed by the cocoa industry is just over 1.2 million—and just under 96 percent of them were not only involved in the production of cocoa but also engaged in work that is very dangerous.[21]

Let us now touch on farmers who grow cocoa within the borders of Ivory Coast. In Ivory Coast, cocoa farmers, according to the Cocoa Barometer (2015), make an average of 50 cents ($0.50) a day. In other words, most Ivorian cocoa farmers, and inevitably their workers, live below the poverty line. There are, as far as I can tell, at least two reasons why the vast majority of cocoa bean farmers earn peanuts. To start with, most if not all cocoa farmers, according to an article for Oxfam America, receive only less than 5 percent of the price of a typical chocolate bar—the rest goes to the chocolate company, the supermarket, and things such as storage, transportation, and marketing.[22]

The second reason, which is probably the most responsible for that depressingly low income, why the average daily income of many a cocoa farmer is not enough to buy a typical chocolate bar is because, in order for them to keep their prices competitive and their farms in business, pretty much all cocoa farmers have to allow the companies that buy their cocoa beans to pay them next to nothing. According to some article, which attributes the following accusation to Ivory Coast's then Prime Minister, chocolate multinationals did something that is without a doubt deepening their already deep pockets (a very simple but clever tactic that, as far as I can see, has either increased the amount of money that they make from the sale of their products, or decreased the prices of their products; and that has dramatically increased and will continue to dramatically increase their profits, either because their piece of the pie is now bigger, or because their chocolates are now cheaper and therefore afforded and bought by more people, and many of the innumerable people who were already consumers of those companies' chocolates on the day that came before the very first day of the implementation of that cunning tactic have definitely increased the amount of chocolate they consume annually): In a word, they, the multinationals in question, encouraged more and more developing countries to grow cocoa.[23] Needless to say, that has dramatically increased the number of cocoa farmers, and, as a result, most if not all cocoa farmers were each forced to lower the already low price of their produce.

Make no mistake, I was by no means trying to defend the innumerable cocoa farmers who have resorted to child labour, which, as if that were not depressing enough, on many a cocoa farm includes many children who have been tricked into slavery by traffickers who have sold them to farmers on whose soil they are now forced to toil. My goal was merely to paint a picture that will hopefully open many a reader's eyes to the forces that have pushed and, sad to say, continues to push innumerable cocoa farmers to resort to some of the worst forms of child labour.

As might have been expected, some of the tasks that are performed on most if not all cocoa farms are backbreaking; and some of them are very dangerous. On a typical workday, innumerable child workers start working their fingers to the bone at six in the morning until the evening, with only a very short lunch break.[24] On most if not all Ivorian cocoa farms, the production of cocoa includes tasks such as clearing the forests with dangerous things such as fire and chainsaws, carrying containers that are each made hundreds if not thousands of times heavier by the cocoa beans with which they are filled, spraying pesticides (which are harmful to human beings, and, in most if not all of the cases in question, are usually or always sprayed without protective gear), and climbing cocoa trees to cut cocoa pods using machetes (large, heavy, dangerous knives, which, for most if not all of the children who work on those farms, are the only tools with which they can or are allowed to extract cocoa beans from the pods). "Holding a single large pod in one hand, each child has to strike the pod with a machete and pry it open with the tip of the blade to expose the cocoa beans. Every strike of the machete has the potential to slice a child's flesh. The majority of children have scars on their hands, arms, legs or shoulders from the machetes."[25] And most of them work 80 to 100 hours per week, make very little or no money at all, and are regularly exhausted, starved, and beaten.[26]

Naturally, when the media exposed the chocolate industry's use of children on cocoa farms, big chocolate companies that use or were using some of the cocoa beans that are or were sourced from cocoa farmers who use child workers were quick to: (1) deny that they knew all along that children are used in the production of cocoa beans; (2) say that their supply chain is so complex that it is impossible for them to know for sure whether or not children were used in the production of the cocoa beans with which they are about to make chocolate; and (3) come up with an initiative whose primary if not only goal is, I believe, to do nothing but give consumers, especially those from whom they regularly make money, the impression that they are against child labour and they care about the welfare of the many millions of poor people who are involved in the production of the cocoa beans with which they make many billions of dollars each and every year.

Allow me to conclude this part of our exploration with a few citations, which, as far as I can see, give substance to my unshakable belief that some if not all of the aforementioned chocolate companies knew all along that children, many of whom were sold to cocoa farmers, are used in the production of cocoa beans.

Among other individuals, the creators of *The Dark Side of Chocolate* interviewed the CEO and owner of SAF-CACAO, a company that is said to (1) be the third-largest cocoa exporter, (2) export to the U.S. and Europe, and (3) make a profit of more than 135 million euros a year. "First of all, there's one thing you should know." Said the CEO. "I was born into the cocoa industry and I have never found children aged 10, 15, 16 or 13 working in a plantation. There are no children in the plantations." Immediately after that, we are shown a secretly filmed cocoa plantation in the north of the Ivory Coast. And other than the cocoa trees all one sees is several children, some of whom are carrying machetes for harvesting the cocoa plants! The documentary then went back to the CEO, who, according to the subtitles, said the following, in addition to what he had recently said, "I can assure the whole world, and not only America and Europe, that the Ivory Coast is a country with no child slaves in the plantations. No children work in the plantations. That has been confirmed. Committees have investigated, and there hasn't been a single report that shows proof of child slavery. Not even at the borders." He was then asked, "So you don't think that the children from Mali and Burkina Faso are being trafficked to the Ivory Coast to work in the cocoa plantations?", and he instantly replied, "No, no, no, no." And then he said, "We are the largest manufacturer. If people don't want to buy cocoa do you know what a disaster that would cause all over the world? Don't play around with words. Get proof. See for yourselves that there are no child slaves in the plantations."

The creators of the documentary then did what he suggested, and when they returned to confront him with their new knowledge, he, believe it or not, changed his tune. After the interviewer told him that "Last time you told me that child labour doesn't exist, but the Interpol has rescued 65 children in an operation," he, according to the subtitles, said, "It's a disaster for the Ivory Coast. It's even in the papers and on TV. One child was found, five children, and those responsible went to jail. So the government is clearly fighting child labor in the plantations."

In addition to opening many a reader's eyes to the illegal use of children by the chocolate industry, I hope to have illustrated that: (1) our economies, and as a result many if not most of us, profit from things such as slavery and child labour, owing to the fact that many if not most of the companies whose profits are dramatically increased by, say, child labour, pay way more tax than they would have had to pay if children were not used in the production of their products or their products' main ingredient; (2) many a consumer of chocolate profits by saving one or two dollars or a few cents whenever they buy chocolate that is made cheap, cheaper, or less expensive by the illegal use of children in the production of cocoa; and (3) millions of business people are each constantly forced to choose between their desire to not be a bad person and their desire to be a good business person, that is to say, to make as much money as they possibly can by maximizing their revenue while minimizing the cost of producing whatever it is that they sell.

Children as Consumers

It goes without saying that our relatively new attitude towards childhood, which is believed by many a scholar to have emerged during the Age of Enlightenment, has played an extremely important role in children's evolution into what they are to innumerable companies, namely, an extremely profitable demographic: children have their own considerable buying power; they influence their parents' buying decisions (where to holiday, where and/or what to eat, which car to buy, et cetera, et cetera); and, needless to say, they are tomorrow's adult consumers.

Because there are trillions of dollars to be made each and every year from purchases by children and the innumerable buying decisions that children will have influenced, countless companies produce advertisements that are aimed specifically at children. And some of those companies each goes so far as to create products not to solve a problem but merely to increase its chances of receiving a portion of the many billions of dollars that some companies make each and every year from and/or with the help of children. Let us touch on only one of the many products that were made by those companies, before we touch on the impact that some of the products that are relentlessly advertised to children have on children.

In response to the dramatic increase of the amount of money that the average parent is willing to spend on their child, many a company that is owned or run by a mercenary, which is someone who is primarily concerned with making money at the expense of ethics, has created at least one product in order to "take advantage of parents' natural desire to provide every possible advantage for their young children." From selling a "training program" called "Your Baby Can Read!" (a set of books, DVDs, flashcards, and a Parent's Guide, which retailed for approximately $200), Dr. Robert Titzer and his company, Infant Learning Company (ILC), are said to have pocketed just under a fifth of a billion US dollars.[27] In addition to the claim that it teaches babies to read, Titzer and ILC claimed that by using that product "during a 'short window of opportunity' starting at three months of age, a child will do better in school and later on in life,"[28] despite the fact that that definitely contradicts some pediatricians' plea for parents to keep their children who are less than 24 months old from watching television or videos, because they strongly believe that watching TV or videos may negatively affect a child's development, owing to the fact that "research links infant screen time to sleep disturbances and delayed language acquisition, as well as problems in later childhood such as poor school performance."[29]

Here are some of the sentences that were printed on the packaging of one of Dr. Titzer's products before he and ILC were finally fined for false advertising: (1)

Early language development system; (2) Starting early is the key to reading success; (3) Give your child the gift of a lifetime; (4) Builds phonics awareness, comprehension, and self-esteem; and (5) Reading system for ages 3 months to 5 years.[30] Apparently, in addition to the aforementioned claims, Titzer and his company claimed that children who used their program could, by the age of three or four, handle reading something as complicated as a Harry Potter book.[31]

Fortunately, "as a result of CCFC's [Campaign for a Commercial-Free Childhood] complaint, the FTC [Federal Trade Commission] took decisive action against Titzer and ILC. The Commission prohibited Titzer and ILC from using the name Your Baby Can Read, or making any claims that their videos had educational benefits unless they produced clear, scientific proof. The FTC also fined Titzer and ILC $186.4 million, most of which was suspended because they were bankrupt." Unfortunately, "Titzer is back, once again peddling digital snake oil and putting babies at risk. There is no evidence that babies learn anything— let alone how to read—by watching videos. And time spent watching videos takes babies away from activities proven to be beneficial, like interacting with caring adults and exploring their surroundings with all their senses."[32]

Now that that is out of the way, let us now touch on junk food, which is probably at the very top of the list of things that are relentlessly marketed to children; some of the negative effects that junk food has on children; and some of the tactics that some companies use or once used in their never-ending collective endeavour to frequently make as much money as they possibly can from children.

But before we do, I would like to remind the reader of the following fact with regard to starvation and many a corporation: As it is the case with adults, it is, needless to say, pretty much impossible for most children who are citizens of an industrialized country to evade starvation without consuming at least one thing that was made by a company or from at least one ingredient that was bought from and/or manufactured by a company. In other words, most of the children who live in industrialized countries "need" (some) companies when it comes to their daily endeavours to ensure that they do not starve to death; not because we cannot evade starvation by simply eating the food that we would have grown and then cooked without the help of companies; but because we, in the interest of the so-called progress, have been persuaded to leave the production and at times the cooking of our food to companies whose owners and employees make a living by exploiting our busyness or laziness and our innate hunger to continue living.

Junk food is, of course, food that contains high levels of calories but has little or no nutritional value. (Because they are derived from food that contains little or no nutrients—protein, vitamins, carbohydrates, and the like, such calories are called "empty calories," and we generally get them from food that has a lot of sugar or other sweeteners and food that has a lot of oil and fat[33].) However, some definitions do not mention the nutritional value of the food. Some people, for example, define *junk food* as "food that is not healthy because it contains a lot of fat, salt, and sugar," (the three pillars on which the food processing industry rests), which Michael Moss, the author of *Salt Sugar Fat: How the Food Giants Hooked Us*, regards as "the Holy Trinity of processed foods."

Included in the list of things that are classified as junk food is, needless to say, things such as pizza, fried chicken, fish and chips, donuts, potato chips, biscuits, ice cream, chocolate, hamburgers, soft drinks, and sugary cereals.

Sad to say, the vast majority of people who consume junk food do not know that many companies that produce junk food go to great pains to ensure that they continue to consume their junk food: they are ignorant of the undeniable fact that—in addition to the many billions of dollars that they spend every single year on marketing campaigns that are brainchildren of people whose main if not only responsibility is to entice as many people who have never tasted their products as possible into tasting them, while they turn as many people who occasionally consume their products as possible into regular consumers of their products—big companies that manufacture junk food spend not a few millions of dollars each and every year on things such as focus groups that are conducted by people whose main if not only responsibility is to make their products addictive or even more addictive and therefore turn consumers of junk food into junk food junkies.

Such companies are relentlessly exploiting our seemingly natural liking for foods that are fatty, salty, and/or sugary. Thanks to the perfect amounts of fat, salt, and sugar, which definitely make their products extremely delicious and thus irresistible, which is without a doubt the main reason why the vast majority of regular consumers of their products consume their products regularly, companies that sell junk food are making a killing selling unhealthy products that have contributed and, sad to say, continue to contribute to many millions of human deaths. Needless to say, the deaths of many millions of people from whom junk food companies used to make money regularly or even each and every day had nothing to do with the effects that junk food had had on their bodies. And that is only because the harmful effects of junk food on our bodies do not always lead to death, and some of those people were each killed by someone or something way or just before the moment during which they would have finally been killed by the disease that was finally brought about by their regular consumption of junk food.

It goes without saying that, like that of those that someone who is a regular consumer of food that has too much salt or too much sugar will in all likelihood be afflicted with someday, the number of diseases that are unwittingly invited into the body of someone who usually eats food that has too much fat is considerable. Indeed, regular consumption of food that has too much fat, salt, or sugar alone will sooner or later have a detrimental effect on one's health. Imagine, if you will, how bad is or was the shape of a body that was for a very long time frequently stuffed with food that had too much fat and too much salt, or too much fat and too much sugar, or too much sugar and too much salt. Now, imagine how bad is or was the shape of a body that was for a very long time frequently stuffed with food that had too much fat, too much salt, and too much sugar.

Before we conclude this part of our exploration, I would like to remind the reader of some of the innumerable diseases that are unwittingly invited into the bodies of people who suffer from obesity, which, as we all know, is one of the many ramifications that are tormenting millions of people whose attitude towards food is or was childish, that is to say, they eat or used to eat primarily or only to please their tongues instead of their bodies: Obesity makes one more likely to have conditions such as gout, diabetes, a heart disease, osteoarthritis (a disease of the joints), high blood pressure, gallbladder disease and gallstones, breathing problems (such as asthma and sleep apnoea, that is, the temporary stoppage of breathing during sleep)[34], and at least 13 cancers (such as thyroid cancer; pancreatic cancer; meningioma, a type of brain tumour that is usually harmless; liver cancer; ovarian cancer; multiple myeloma, a type of blood cancer; gallbladder cancer; and postmenopausal breast cancer)[35]. As Hippocrates, a Greek physician who is traditionally regarded as the father of medicine, is said to have written, "Corpulence is not only a disease itself, but the harbinger of others."

Finally, let us now touch on a few of the many ploys that not a few junk food companies are implementing or once implemented in order to contribute to their own never-ending collective endeavour to dramatically increase the number of children from whom and/or from whose parents they are making a lot of money.

Let us start with the most obvious: Some companies that sell junk food, companies such as McDonald's, use "free" toys to lure young children into their restaurants. Their cunningness aside, the person who came up with that idea, which probably turned out to be hundreds of thousands if not millions of times more profitable than they had expected or hoped, is, as far as I can see, a marketing genius. I mean, pretty much every young child loves toys, and, as we all know, when you are hungry, food, especially meals that have a lot of fat, salt, and/or sugar, is irresistible. Now, imagine how irresistible a Happy Meal that is accompanied by a "free" cartoon character such as SpongeBob SquarePants is to someone who is not only a few years old but also troubled by hunger, which is, whenever it visits a child, hardly ever accompanied by a craving for healthy food.

Junk food companies are, of course, not the only companies that make many millions of dollars each and every year from the exploitation of some children's love for some cartoon characters: innumerable companies use them to sell things such as clothing, lunchboxes, school bags, toys, and duvets to young children.

There are, of course, other things that one could say about some companies' exploitation of some children's love for toys and cartoons through the use of toys and cartoon characters. Some people, for example, are of the conviction that some companies create or once created television programs for young children for the sole purpose of selling toys to them—toys that are or were, needless to say, for the most part made up of the main characters of those television programs. Another example: Creators of some television programs, movies, comics books, and video games whose main characters were turned into action figures market toys that "promote violence and revenge as a way of life" to young children, the vast majority of whom are without a doubt boys. (Believe it or not, although I know not a few of them, the number of superheroes that I know who, without the use of violence, stop villains from continuing to do evil things does not exceed zero.) Having said that, instead of saying more than is necessary, I am going to end this part about the use of toys to sell junk food to young children by sharing some of the facts that I have discovered while writing this part of this book. And to do that, I am going to simply cite a few extracts from a relevant documentary.

Santa's Workshop: Inside China's Slave Labour Toy Factories (2004) starts with the following questions to and answers from an anonymous factory worker: "How many days a week do you work?" *"Seven days. We start half past six in the morning and work till midnight. Then we do overtime work until two or four a.m."* "What toys are produced at the factory?" *"Dolls and dogs for Disney."* And then we, after a second or two, are shown three factory workers working next to a pile of Mickey Mouse dolls. Just over a minute and half after that, a teenage boy says the following: "When I was younger I found out that McDonald's toys were made by children. After that I didn't want those toys anymore, since children made them. I thought adults or machines made them." His remark is followed by the following remark by the narrator: "In August 2000, it was revealed that one of the factories making toys for McDonald's employed child labour. The factory was situated in China, where most of the world's toys are made."

That was the first ploy. Let us now touch on another one of the many ploys with which some companies once attempted or are attempting to dramatically increase the already substantial number of children who consume their products.

When it comes to children, loyalty to the McDonald's brand is, of course, patiently instilled through things such as Ronald McDonald, a clown character that McDonald's uses as its primary mascot, and Happy Meals, a form of kids' meals that are each accompanied by a toy for boys or girls. Anyway, the McDonald's restaurants in Seminole County, a county in the state of Florida, once implemented a ploy whose primary if not only purpose was, I believe, to gradually turn as many children as they possibly could into loyal customers of McDonald's: through a cunning report card incentive program of theirs, they, during the 2007 to 2008 school year, rewarded elementary school students whose attendance or grades were good with Happy Meals. Although there were many people who were upset by the undeniable fact that that program allowed McDonald's to cunningly link its brand with academic performance, that, as far as

I can see, is not what led to the backlash that eventually pressured McDonald's executives into removing McDonald's "trademarks from report-card jackets in Seminole County." That backlash was, I believe, caused by the fact that—because they had paid the bill ($1,600) for the printing costs associated with 27,000 students' report cards[36]—the McDonald's restaurants in question printed Ronald McDonald, the Golden Arches logo, and a photograph of Happy Meal menu items on the report-card jacket, which the Florida elementary schools' students use throughout the entire school year.[37] What's more, McDonald's, believe it or not, had already pledged to stop advertising to children under 12. Or rather, McDonald's had already pledged to stop targeting children who are under the age of 12 with advertisements whose goal is to seduce them into eating meals or snacks that do not meet certain nutritional guidelines.

Let us now, as our third ploy, touch on one of the ideas that, in addition to making a lot of money for them, betray the cunningness of some companies.

In its attempt to milk some parents' natural desire to provide every possible advantage for their young children, a company that manufactures Cheerios (a brand of cereal) has, with the help of a publisher, created a series of "play books," which have the word "Cheerios" in their names (*The Cheerios Animal Play Book*, *The Cheerios Halloween Play Book*, *The Cheerios Christmas Play Book*, etc.) and cannot be used as per those two companies' cunning plan if a child does not have Cheerios cereal. Here is how the creators of those "play books," which have "Fill in the missing Cheerios!" printed on their front covers, want young children to use them: *The Cheerios Play Book* has the following sentences on its back cover, "*Bring your own Cheerios!* On every page, there are pictures that need to be completed by adding Cheerios to just the right places. (No milk, please!) Teddies need Cheerios buttons, mice need Cheerios glasses, and fish need Cheerios bubbles. Pages are recessed to help children successfully place their own dry cereal pieces within the scenes. *Tasty, interactive fun that toddlers will love!*"

Without a doubt, that, from a business standpoint, is commendable. I mean, (1) chances are that every now and then the company that manufactures Cheerios makes a significant amount of money from the sale of those books—that ploy is or would still be profitable if or even if that company isn't or weren't making money from the sale of those books, because (2) come the day on which they will have been published for 30 years, those books, because they artfully cause their users to associate Cheerios with fun and learning, will have dramatically increased the number of children and parents who are loyal to the Cheerios brand; (3) for a child to be able to use any of those books as per their creators' cunning plan, their parent needs to buy and always have at least one box of Cheerios; and (4) many of the children who that will have molded into loyal consumers of Cheerios will someday buy Cheerios and/or at least one of those "play books" for their own children.

Because I have already touched on some of the harmful effects that regular consumption of junk food has on our bodies, I am not going to bore the reader by mentioning some of the diseases that are now tormenting gazillions of people who are or used to be regular consumers of cereals that either contain a lot of sugar, or taste like cardboard when eaten without having added a lot of sugar to them. I am simply going to share the following facts: (1) not a few people have Honey Nut Cheerios on their lists of "Breakfast Cereals to Avoid"[38]; and (2) at least one person is of the conviction that Cheerios Protein Oats & Honey are "one of the most toxic cereals that you should NOT be feeding your child."[39]

The aforementioned "play books" are by no means the only products with which the company that manufactures Cheerios is attempting to educate or at least entertain young children while it is patiently and cunningly impressing some of its products' names and logos on their minds. Like the company that manufactures Froot Loops and the one that manufactures M&M's, to name but a few, the company that manufactures Cheerios produces or once produced "counting books." On top of a very colourful illustration, the very first set of two pages of *The Oreo Cookie Counting Book* has the following maths problem: "10 little OREOs all in a line. Dunk one in a glass of milk, and now there are ..."; the second: "9 little OREOs stacked on a plate. Twist one open, and then there are ..."

Before we move on to the penultimate ploy, I would

like to cite two reviews of *The Oreo Cookie Counting Book* in order to show the reader that some parents, unlike some activists, do not, believe it or not, see anything wrong with such ploys: (1) "Kids get bombarded at every angle with the message that junk food is fun, kid-friendly, and harmless. Now it's educational? I would run, not walk, from any book like this. If you want your kid to count food, at least pick something nutritious. There's no need to line Nabisco's pockets at the expense of your children's health. They'll get the junk food message everywhere else—let's at least try to keep it out [of] our children's books."; and (2) "This is a cute book that is very sturdy (glossy surfaced card board). The Oreo design adds to the fun."[40]

Because I still cannot explain this as lucidly as it has, even though I have tried innumerable times, I will, for this ploy, simply cite Campaign for a Commercial-Free Childhood's explanation of and stance on the following ploy by McDonald's: "**What are McTeacher's Nights?** Events McDonald's calls 'McTeacher's Nights' are part of a comprehensive marketing strategy McDonald's has developed to target children wherever they are, including in schools. On McTeacher's

Nights, McDonald's enlists teachers as brand ambassadors to sell the corporation's junk food to students and students' families. At the events, McDonald's invites teachers and school administrators to 'work' behind McDonald's store counters, wear branded uniforms, and serve burgers, fries, and sugary drinks to their students and students' families. In exchange for the kind of marketing that money can't buy, McDonald's contributes only a small percentage of the events' proceeds to schools. **What's wrong with McTeacher's Nights?** During McTeacher's Nights, McDonald's exploits cash-strapped schools to market its brand and its fast food to children. The events encourage students to eat junk food, undermining the hard work that parents, teachers, and administrators do to promote healthy habits for children. Parents and students trust teachers to do what's best for students' health. By enlisting teachers to market junk food to kids, McDonald's manipulates that trust. In the midst of one of the largest preventable health crises in the U.S.—one that is closely linked to diet and increasingly affects children—it's deeply irresponsible for McDonald's to exploit limited school budgets to market fast food to children. **Do McTeacher's Nights help schools?** McTeacher's Night events are poor fundraisers that bring very little revenue to the schools that participate. Schools generally receive only 15 to 20 percent of the proceeds from each event. A survey conducted by Campaign for a Commercial-Free Childhood and Corporate Accountability International revealed that schools receive, on average, just $1.18 per student. *One high school in 2014 earned just five cents per student.* McTeacher's Nights promote McDonald's food and its brand, but these events offer little for schools, and fall far short of the kind of philanthropy McDonald's claims they provide."[41]

Finally, let us now, as our very last ploy, touch on a cunning initiative by Cadbury, which is, of course, one of the largest confectionery brands in the world.

As its primary endeavour to clean its image, Cadbury came up with yet another initiative whose main if not only objective seems to me to be to associate itself with a healthy lifestyle. Needless to say, among other cunning things, some junk food companies, in their relentless endeavours to create or preserve that extremely profitable association, make athletes their ambassadors and/or sponsor professional sports events such as the Olympics and the FIFA World Cup (the latter alone has, of course, put some junk food companies' logos and/or marketing messages in front of many billions of people around the world, many millions of whom are without a doubt children, many of whom are very young).

In 2003, Cadbury launched a marketing scheme called Cadbury Get Active, which Cadbury, believe it or not, regarded as its contribution to the fight against obesity—by increasing or improving physical exercise in Britain's primary and secondary schools. The scheme encouraged children to collect vouchers, which could be found only on wrappers of some of the chocolate bars that Cadbury manufactures, in exchange for "free" sports equipment for their school. Parents were also encouraged to take part in the scheme in question by collecting tokens on wrappers of chocolate bars such as Flake and Crunchie and then exchanging them for "free" sports equipment for their local primary or secondary school.[42]

It goes without saying that that alone is sickening. But, believe it or not, that is not all. According to The

Food Commission, an independent watchdog that is campaigning for healthier food in Britain, to collect enough chocolate wrappers that would get them a set of volleyball net posts, which were the most expensive item that Cadbury offered, a school had to encourage its students to spend over two thousand British pounds on chocolate bars, which have nearly 1.25 million calories. What's more, this ploy was endorsed by the British government, and, if British school children had purchased all of the 160 million tokens that Cadbury had planned to issue, they, in their pitiful endeavour to burn fat, would have purchased and probably consumed almost two million kilograms of fat![43]

As might have been expected, not only are many if not most junk food companies denying that the products with which they make not a few millions of dollars each and every day are among the things that have caused and are now sustaining if not worsening the obesity epidemic, they, when it comes to overweight children, are blaming parents for not watching what their children eat, and the children's sedentary lifestyles and their overindulgence.

Here are some of the things that, I believe, have

contributed the most to the obesity epidemic: (1) the average human being's ignorance of the undeniable fact that pretty much all processed foods contain added sugar; and in the nature of things (2) most of us have absolutely no idea how much sugar we are consuming each and every day; (3) when it comes to the part of their "nutrition facts" labels that is supposed to tell us how much added sugar they have put in their products, many food processing companies, especially those who manufacture junk food, use, probably as an attempt to keep a secret the sugariness of their products, terms such as anhydrous dextrose, cane crystals, corn sweetener, corn syrup, crystal dextrose, fruit juice concentrates, and molasses[44], which, needless to say, the average consumer does not know what they are; (4) most of us do not know that some fruit juices, such as orange juice, have roughly the same amount of sugar as soda.[45]; and (5) the preposterous yet quite common misbelief that, when it comes to fruit juice, "100%" means "low in sugar" or "sugar-free."

Obviously, to the second culprit one can add the undeniable fact that, because they do not know that (about) 4 grams of sugar is equivalent to one teaspoon of granulated sugar[46], the vast majority of literate people who consume processed foods cannot convert the number of grams of sugar or sugars that is printed on a "nutrition facts" label into teaspoons of granulated sugar in order for them to get an idea of how much sugar is in the product; and the unfortunate fact that most of us do not even know what is the maximum amount of sugar that, according to many an expert, one can consume each and every day without inevitably inviting diseases that many millions of people have unwittingly invited into their bodies by regularly consuming too much sugar, especially added sugars, which innumerable people regard as "the single worst ingredient in the modern diet."

According to a scientific statement that is said to be published in *Circulation*, a journal by the American Heart Association (AHA), children aged 2 to 18 should eat or drink less than 6 teaspoons of added sugars (which is equivalent to about 25 grams or 100 calories) per day.[47] In order to decrease the depressingly large number of people who have absolutely no idea how much added sugars are consumed each and every day by many millions of children, many of whom are very young, allow me to share the following facts: (1) According to The Coca-Cola Company, a 355ml can of Coke has 39 grams or just under 10 teaspoons of sugars, whereas a 500ml bottle of Coke has over 52 grams of sugars,[48] that is to say, over 12 teaspoons of added sugars, which is, of course, more than twice the maximum amount of added sugars that, according to the AHA, can be safely consumed daily by children aged 2 to 18 (speaking of Coke, not only do I know a handful of people who each drinks at least 2 litres of Coke— which has about 53 teaspoons of added sugars—pretty much every day, I used to be one of them); and (2) a 60g 3 Musketeers chocolate bar has just over 40 grams of added sugars[49], while a 61.5g bag of Skittles Original Fruit has 46 grams of added sugars.[50]

Needless to say, in addition to the fact that a glass of fruit juice or soft drink (which some people call soda) is one of the innumerable things that are loaded with added sugars and are consumed by innumerable millions of children pretty much every day, a depressingly large number of children, in addition to other processed foods that are loaded with added sugars, each consumes, say, a glass of orange juice or soft drink and, say, a chocolate bar such as 3 Musketeers and/or a bag of sweets such as Skittles, pretty much every day. In other words, hundreds of thousands if not millions of children each consumes, every two or three months, added sugars whose amount is way more than the maximum amount of added sugars that they, according to the AHA, can safely consume each and every year.

Indeed, even most if not all of the people who strongly believe that the health of the vast majority of human beings is less important than the wealth of a relatively small number of shareholders agree that, while most of the things that make some parts of our lives way easier, safer, or better than some parts of some of our ancestors' lives (things such as clothing, condoms, vehicles, morning-after pills, prosthetics, and sanitary pads) are without a doubt manufactured or provided by companies, the vast majority of the negative impacts that human beings have had on the environment and other human beings are attributable to companies' extraction of raw materials, companies' manufacturing processes, things that are or used to be manufactured by companies, which manufacture or used to manufacture them mainly if not only to make as much money as they possibly can or could, and, needless to say, companies' relentless endeavours to sell as many products of theirs or their clients' as they possibly can or could.

The Use of Children by Children

Many a child is, needless to say, frequently used by many a child. Among other things, many a child uses many a child as: (1) a creature to whose toy (or school bag, cellphone, car, etc.) they sometimes direct their parents' attention in order to dramatically increase their chances of managing to persuade their parents to buy them a toy (or school bag, cellphone, car, etc.) that is the same as, similar to, or better than the one or the ones that belong to the other child or children; (2) a playmate with whom they sometimes attempt to evade boredom while they endure socialization, that is, the process during which their parents, teachers, and others transform them into socially and cultur-ally adept creatures; the process during which, since we are born without any culture, children adopt the norms of their culture and learn things such as the roles they are to play in their societies[51]; (3) a plaything with which they sometimes kill time while they are waiting for their parents to finally exit their employers' yards ... or their bedroom; and/or (4) an object of their bullying, which they sometimes do to, among other things, get attention, make themselves popular, and/or conceal their shame or boost their self-esteem, since demeaning others makes them feel empowered[52].

The Use of Children by Adults

That the manner in which and the purposes for which some adults use some children differ from culture to culture goes without saying. For example, where I grew up, like most if not all of the other parts of South Africa, adults sometimes ask, or rather command, children, most of whom are not even theirs, to do for them things that they are too busy, old, sick, tired, or lazy to do. Things such as: (1) taking something to or from their neighbour's house or yard; (2) going to buy things such as a cigarette, a loaf of bread, and a bottle of beer; and (3) going to ask their neighbour if they have a few teaspoons or about half a cup of sugar that they do not mind not having for a few hours, days, weeks ... or even months.

Having said that, there are many ways in which adults use children that are common in most countries. Many an adult, for example, sometimes uses a child or children to make themselves feel or seem like they are either a good person, or at least not as bad as some people strongly believe they are, by giving the child or children things such as money and sweets, even if they did not ask for it or them.

The Use of Children by Grandparents

According to some people's interpretation of the first half of Proverbs 17:6, that is, "Grandchildren are the crown of the aged," grandchildren are beautiful jewels that are worn like strings of pearls by their grandparents.[53] Naturally, I have not a few things to say with regard to retirement and the intense boredom that is tormenting pretty much all sane retirees. Having said that, because there are still many things to touch on, I will, instead of doing that, simply cite a few aphorisms of mine from *N for Nigger*, my very first collection of aphorisms: (1) "Retirement is a stage where an employer discards an employee that he cannot exploit further." (2) "Artists do not retire; they die." (3) "Retirement is the menopause of an employee's mind and hands." (4) "Grandchildren are their grandparents' toys." and (5) "As a subconscious attempt to add meaning or a sense of purpose to their lives, the unemployed pray for jobs; the retired pray for grandchildren."

The Use of Children by Parents

Sad to say, I cannot, needless to say, enumerate each and every manner in which and every single purpose for which parents use their children. But, fortunately for me, doing that is by no means necessary. I will, because of that, share only the uses that, in addition to not being unaware of them, I cannot conclude this part of our exploration without having touched on them and still not hate myself.

Some parents are, of course, by no means "guilty" of some of the following common uses of children. What's more, most if not all of the parents who will have read what I am about to assert will readily exclude themselves from the group that is made up of many a person who uses or has used their child or children in their endeavour to achieve at least one of the following ends. As far as I can see, that is because what I am about to "accuse" pretty much all parents of will leave many if not most parents with a pang of shame, and/or because some of the following cravings, which many a sane human being has, are, I believe, subconscious; that is to say, the cravings have influenced many a parent's feelings and actions, even though he or she is not or was not aware of their presence.

Finally, this part of our exploration is by no means irrelevant to readers who are not parents. (I mean, in addition to the fact that many millions of sane people who are not parents want to be parents someday, each and every person is some people's child; that is to say, every person has or had parents, who probably made them because of at least one of the following reasons why many billions of sane human beings have reproduced or will reproduce intentionally.) As a matter of fact, this part was written primarily for people who do not have children. Which means that I would definitely choose the second option if I had to choose between this part being read by one million parents and it being read by one nonparent.

Wasted Wombs and Sperms

The main reason why some people have reproduced is because they can or they could. In other words, they reproduce or have reproduced mainly because, as I have said earlier, they each have or had the ability to produce children (with, needless to say, the pivotal help of a fertile male or female), and they strongly believe or believed that they are or were blessed with that for a reason. In a word, they each became a parent primarily because they did not want to let their fertility go to waste, and becoming a parent was and is the only way to avoid that.

The Comfort of Conformity

To the vast majority of sane parents whose firstborns were not made by mistake, bringing at least one child into this troubled world of ours is without a doubt one of the many things that they each had to do in order to avoid one of the many things that they, like most sane human beings, are forever moving heaven and earth to avoid, namely, being regarded as a failure, abnormal, or insane. Among other reasons, as I have asserted earlier, many if not most sane parents have reproduced because most sane human beings have either reproduced or attempted to do so, are attempting to reproduce, or would love to reproduce someday. And what better way to come across as sane, or to prove that you are, than to do what most sane human beings have done or plan on doing someday?

Being In God's Good Books

A few pages ago, I have asserted that, among other reasons, some people have intentionally become parents because they are or were of the unshakable belief that God has clearly commanded the human race, or rather human beings who He did not curse or bless with infertility, to reproduce. In the nature of things, I am of the unshakable belief that becoming a parent is one of the gazillions of things that most sane human beings strongly believe that one has to do or realize in order for one to be or to remain in God's good books, which is believed by many if not most believers to be the only route that will get one through the gates of heaven.

Indeed, in innumerable instances, the main or the only real reason why the boyfriend and his girlfriend, the sex partners, or the one-night stands became parents, even though they both did not want a child at that time, is because becoming parents was the only route through which they could evade abortion, which, according to one of many if not most believers' unshakable beliefs, makes God's blood boil. In other words, many millions of pregnancies—many if not most of which have each led to the birth of at least one child—were each used as nothing but a conspicuous means to a secret end called the evasion of abortion.

And that is by no means limited to unmarried people. I personally know a couple who, a few months after their wedding day, reluctantly decided to become parents a few years before the year during which they had planned on having their firstborn; not only because the contraceptive that they were using at that time had just disappointed them but also because they did not want to disappoint God by returning the fetus to (Him, the being they believe is) the sender (of things such as fetuses). What's more, chances are that there are innumerable married people who, because they believe that God is against abortion, have each decided to not abort the fetus that is an end result of an instance of unprotected sex between them and the person with whom they are cheating or once cheated on their wife ... or husband. (Yes, they probably knew that adultery is unbiblical!)

Please Thy Father and Thy Mother

The average sane person, as we all know, has an extremely powerful desire to win other sane people's approval, particularly those who he or she knows and/ or from whose approval he or she is likely to benefit. Needless to say, their parent or parents are among the people who are at the very top of the list that is made up of sane people whose approval the average sane person wants or wanted to win.

I believe that regardless of how much money they make or have made, or how positively they contribute or have contributed to the human race, many if not most sane parents, if truth be told, would not have won their parents' approval, if they—to borrow one of the many interpretations of the first half of Proverbs 17:6—had not given their parents "beautiful jewels" that they, their children's grandparents, wear or wore "like strings of pearls." In other words, they would not have won their parents' approval if they had not become parents themselves.

What's more, innumerable sane adults who are or seem too old to become parents are each openly or secretly regarded as a disgrace to their parent or parents, by not only some of the sane human beings who know them but also their very own parent or parents.

Lending a Small Helping Hand

It goes without saying that there are many ways in which parents use their own children as helpers. Be that as it may, because doing that is not necessary, I will not touch on all of the many uses of children as helpers by their own parents.

Anyway, let us touch on only a few of them: (1) Gazillions of parents use their own children as unpaid domestic workers whenever their domestic workers are not on duty, or because they do not have domestic workers; (2) Many a child is expected or forced to do some of the chores that are usually done by maids in most households that have maids, even when their parents' maid is on duty; (3) Millions of children are sometimes used by their own parents as babysitters, and, whenever that happens, many of them are each required to look after more than one child at a time.

Speaking of babysitting, I strongly believe that a significant number of children who used to be used or are sometimes used by their own parents as babysitters have unwittingly contributed to the survival of the human race and the size of the human population, because many an instance where a couple had just asked or ordered their eldest child or children to look after their youngest child or children while they, the parents, went to some place to secretly attempt to make yet another child without disturbance from their other child or children has led or will lead to the birth of at least one child; (4) Millions of children have each been asked or ordered by their own parent or parents to accept a job offer or to look for a job so that they, the child, will be able to regularly contribute to their family's daily endeavour to evade starvation and/or homelessness. Obviously, in countless households the children are the only ones who are working only because their parents are unemployed or too sick or too old to work; and (5) whenever they are begging for food and/or money, hundreds of thousands if not millions of parents each uses his or her own child or children's presence as a desperate means to dramatically increase the number of passersby who will have given him or her food and/or money by the time he or she stops begging for the day.

Children as Private Property

One of the main reasons why some people have intentionally become parents is because they enjoy (or used to enjoy) and/or they love (or used to love) children, and, like most sane human beings of today, they cannot or could not really enjoy and/or love something or someone without desiring to have it or them; otherwise many of them would have seen the countless children to whom they have access as more than enough instead of them producing children of their own.

Needless to say, that attitude, which is definitely based on a misbelief, is of crucial importance to the development and success of pretty much all countries' economies. As a matter of fact, the world economy would collapse if a significant number of people were to realize and then act on the realization that it is possible to enjoy many if not most of the things that they enjoy without first having to own them. Anyway, that attitude towards people and things is inevitably shared by pretty much all sane human beings whose society is based on private property. Not only do those people "need" to possess someone or something in order for them to or because they enjoy and/or love that person or that thing, they, in the nature of things, also regard the children to whom they are parents as "theirs."

Make no mistake, there are, as I have just implied, people who do not suffer from that childish attitude. As Kahlil Gibran is said to have written in "On Children," which is found in *The Prophet*, "Your children are not your children. They are the sons and daughters of Life's longing for itself. They come through you but not from you, and though they are with you yet they belong not to you."

Wise Children and Depressed Psychiatrists

Many a parent has used or will use their child as a

second chance: an opportunity for them, the parent, to choose what they strongly believe they should have chosen a few or many years ago when they had to choose. To choose, for example, right instead of left ... or wrong, pleasing parents and schoolteachers instead of pleasing friends, love instead of money, self-employment instead of employment, character instead of looks, education instead of love life, mortgage instead of rental, obscurity instead of fame, brains instead of beauty, lover instead of family, art school instead of law school, family instead of money, or vice versa.

To be sure, in some instances the child would have been better off and happy or happier than they are if, instead of what they have chosen, they had chosen what their parents had advised or commanded them to choose. Having said that, following their parents' advice or doing what their parents have commanded them to do has left innumerable people worse off and unhappy or unhappier than they were. In the nature of things, countless people, needless to say, each hate the path that their parent or parents have recommended or forced them to choose.

Because of that, I believe that in many instances

the child does not value or enjoy the fruits that are produced by the path that his or her parents have advised or commanded him or her to choose, and many of those who do do not value or enjoy them as much as their parents do. And that is, of course, because many a parent, sad to say, has used their child as an opportunity for them, the parent, to do, through their child, something or some of the things that they, the parent, did not do or did not do successfully. As we all know, many a person would definitely not be a doctor or a lawyer if their parent had not advised or commanded them to study medicine or law. What's more, their parent would have not done that if they, the parent, were not eluded by their dream of being a doctor or a lawyer.

The Trophy Child

For this part of our exploration I will simply quote a definition of *trophy child*, which is "a child whose birth or achievements are paraded to enhance the parents' status." As far as I can see, the following are some of the reasons why those two things enhance the parents' status, or why they are believed to do that: (1) In many a case, the child's birth has transformed or will transform the couple into a family, which is, as we all know, one of the things that many if not most sane human beings value the most, and are moving, have moved, or will move heaven and earth to each be a co-founder of one; and (2) As is the case with the parent or parents in such a case, many if not most of the people in front of whom a child's achievements are paraded strongly believe that it is impossible for a child whose parents are bad parents to achieve something that is worth parading.

Trapped into Marriage

Among other reasons, some people got married so that they can reproduce without disappointing their parents, their church members, and God, whereas some people have each persuaded or tricked their partner into making at least one child with them in order to increase their chances of being the person to whom their partner will get married someday. If their partner will get married someday, that is. Granted, some people would have still married their partners even if they did not have children with them, but some people would not be married to their spouses if they did not have children with them. As a matter of fact, many of them would not be married to anyone if they did not have children.

Children as Cement

Getting married is without a doubt not the only thing that some people have each done primarily or only as a desperate attempt of theirs to dramatically decrease their chances of being left by the person to whom they are or used to be married. Interestingly enough, not getting married has in countless cases resulted in the opposite: gazillions of men were left by their then girlfriends merely because they do not want to ever get married, or because they did not want to or could not get married then. Anyway, here is another deed with which millions of people have each attempted to dramatically increase their chances of not being left by their partner: The primary or only reason why some people have each asked or begged their partner to make a baby with them is because they believe that sharing parenthood with their partner will increase their own chances of remaining their partner till death do them part, or until they no longer love or want their partner.

Having said that, as is definitely the case with marrying them, having a child with someone, needless to say, does not necessarily mean that they will never leave you, or that you will never leave them: not a few millions of people, as we all know, were each left by the person to whom they were married and/or with whom they had or have a child, a few children, or not a few children.

In short, some of us were brought into this troubled world primarily or only to increase our fathers' chances of not being left by our mothers, or vice versa.

Make no mistake, hundreds of thousands if not millions of relationships would have been ended a long time ago if they had not produced children. In gazillions of instances, the child or children's existence make it difficult or even "impossible" for their parents to end their marriage or relationship. "I don't regret having my kids but they sure make it difficult to leave my wife." Some man has anonymously complained online. "If it weren't for them I would have left a long time ago."[54]

Former Partners' Pawns

In addition to having used them in her then endeavour to increase her then boyfriend or sex partner's chances of getting married and her chances of being the woman to whom he would be married, many a woman is using her child or children to control their father to whom she is no longer married. Although I am about to share only one, there are without a doubt more than one way in which children are used to control their fathers. (Allow me to borrow yet another aphorism of mine from *N for Nigger*.) In a word, "While still lovers: to control her man, a woman uses (the man's access to) her vagina. When ex-lovers: she uses (the man's access to) their kids." What's more, many a divorced parent has become or is pretending to have become a better parent in order for them to be able to use their child or children as a pawn or pawns in a very popular childish game called Make Your Ex Wish They Had Not Left You ... or Allowed You to Leave Them.

Money Can't Buy You Children

Another common yet narrowly known purpose for which children are used is to humble people who want but cannot have children, particularly those who flaunt their prosperity and/or are arrogant. "Life humbles the rich," as I have asserted elsewhere, "by giving them problems that money cannot dissolve or resolve."

A Mountain of Things

One of the many reasons why many a child was intentionally brought into this troubled world of ours is because their parents didn't or don't want the money and the possessions that they have or will have amassed to be inherited by someone who is not a product or byproduct of a particular instance of unprotected sex in which either or both of them took part. As we all know, in addition to forever moving mountains to amass as much money and as many possessions as they possibly can, millions of sane people are of the unshakable belief that it would be foolish of them to toil almost daily for many years only to leave the remaining fruits of their toil with someone else's child or children. (That, by the way, is, as far as I can see, one of the main reasons why many if not most people take a dim view of adoption). Which means that, among other reasons, many a couple has reproduced in order to avoid leaving the money and the possessions that it will have amassed, come the very first day on which both partners will be dead, with someone who is not (or people who are not) the couple's biological child (or children) lest the partners be regarded as fools.

THE USE AND MISUSE OF CHILDREN

The Preservation of Surnames, Beliefs, and Ideas

It goes without saying that, in this patrilineal society of ours, the number of people whose surname is
Mokhonoana would in the long run be less than one
if each and every male who is so surnamed were to be
castrated. Which, needless to say, means that, among
other reasons, many a male was brought into this
troubled world of ours in order to increase or at least
maintain the number of sane people—particularly fertile males—who have the very same surname as him.

Let us now touch on the preservation of beliefs:
Some children were intentionally brought into this
troubled world of ours because, among other things,
their parents want to preserve some or all of their
cherished beliefs (many if not most of which they, the
parents, got from their own parents, the children's
grandparents) by passing them on to their own children (who, needless to say, will probably pass all or
some of those beliefs and the baton on to their own
children someday).

The same can, of course, be said about ideas and
ideals. By the way, the seed that has grown and ma-

tured into this book was unwittingly planted by a friend of mine six or so years ago. After he had passionately told me that we should not make the mistake of not becoming parents, I asked him why, and he said that, I paraphrase, so that our ideas will not be buried or cremated with us.

A Boost to a Patriarch's Ego

Like their mother's, many a child's presence gives their father an opportunity for him to give someone orders in a domineering manner like and as frequently as he is given orders in a domineering manner by his own boss—that, as far as I can see, dramatically increases their fathers' chances of tolerating their bossy bosses instead of telling them to go to hell or to each go make love to themselves. As a result, those children, like their mothers, benefit from the fruits of being given orders in a domineering manner by their fathers, seeing that they each belong to a nuclear family that is headed by a man who, thanks to the role they play in question, still has a job.

To sum up, allow me to share yet another aphorism of mine, which will be placed somewhere between the front and the back cover of a book that I plan on publishing as my second collection of aphorisms in a few months' time (if I will still be alive, that is): "In a patriarchal society, one of the most important functions of the institution of the family is to make feel like a somebody whenever he is in his own yard a man who is a nobody whenever he is in his employer's yard."

Speaking of parents' egos, I would not forgive myself if I were to write this book's very last sentence without having shared the following observation, which is said to have been written by Jarod Kintz: "The best part about having children is being able to point at them and proudly proclaim, 'Hey, I made those.'"

Children as an Index of Prosperity

In addition to dramatically increasing their child's chances of being better educated and thus better paid than some or preferably all of the children whose parents grew up with, live nearby, and/or hate the child's parent (which will definitely make the child's parent seem to many sane people to be a better parent than those children's parents), many a parent has sent their child to a private and very expensive school in order to give people who know the parent an idea of how deep the parent's pockets are (if the parent, unlike most people, has a lot of money), or what and how much the parent is willing to sacrifice for the sake of their child's future (if the parent, like most people, does not have a lot of money).

Educational institutions are, of course, not the only things that millions of parents have used, use, or will use in their never-ending endeavours to each leave as many sane people as they possibly can with the impression that they, the parents, are good parents unlike many parents or better parents than most parents. Instead of or in addition to those institutions, millions of parents use things such as the toys with which their children evade boredom and the clothes with which their children evade nudity. Things such as expensive toys and overpriced clothes, as we all know, are also used by not a few millions of parents in their never-ending endeavours to each leave as many sane people as they possibly can, particularly those who hate them and those with whom they each used to be in a relationship, with the impression that they, the parents, are very prosperous.

Needless to say, some of the parents who (through the use of one, some, or all of the aforementioned things) have managed to leave some people with the impression that they, the parents, are prosperous are not prosperous. Indeed, the same can be said about some of the parents who (through the use of one, some, or all of the aforementioned things) have managed to leave some people with the impression that they, the parents, are good parents. If regularly spending a lot of money on one's child is not a prerequisite for being a good parent, that is.

To benefit from either or both of those impressions, all that those parents needed was for those "spectators" to truly believe that they, the parents, are prosperous and/or good parents. As I have asserted elsewhere: a misbelief, like a lie, can be as profitable as or even more profitable than a fact. First example: During an "armed" robbery, a toy gun need not be "real" for it to cause cashiers to open their tills—all that the robber needs is for the cashiers to believe that it is. Second example: When selecting a one-night stand, a heterosexual woman who is materialistic is a trillion times more likely to choose a sexually unattractive poor man who seems rich over a sexually attractive rich man who seems poor.

Children as Their Parents' Foster Parents

One of the most common reasons why many a person has intentionally become a parent is because, like most sane human beings, they are terrified of loneliness, and at that time they strongly believed that the number of times that they will have been lonely as a retiree come the day during which they are going to kick the bucket will have been dramatically minimized by their having a child or children, who they openly or secretly hope will have children of their own way before then.

In the nature of things, loneliness tortures many if not most of the elderly more intensely and more frequently than it torments many if not most of us who

will never be or have not yet been pushed or pulled
into old age. Perhaps that is because, among other
reasons, the average elderly person: (1) is unable to do
some of the things that they used to be able to do for
themselves by themselves; (2) has buried most of the
people to whom they were related and/or very close;
(3) was not born into, did not cofound, or is no longer
part of a large nuclear family; and (4) was pushed or
pulled out of employment, which—for a few decades
for about eight hours pretty much all weekdays—used
to keep them too busy to become lonely or to entertain
their loneliness.

That said, because I strongly believe that my asser-
tion that grandchildren are their grandparents' toys is
still in the reader's mind, and that the reader is sharp-
witted, I am not going to touch on how many a person
has, I believe, contributed to their parent or parents'
frequent endeavour or endeavours to evade boredom
and loneliness.

Let us, in order to get to the point, link parenting
one's parent or parents with the first of the aforementioned reasons (to which I have attributed my conviction that loneliness torments the average elderly

person more intensely and more frequently than it tortures the average person who has not yet lived that long): Many if not most of the many millions of people who have intentionally become parents became parents because, in addition to many other objectives, they each wanted to dramatically increase their chances of having a caregiver that was conceived in their womb or with the help of their sperm, should they be fortunate or unfortunate enough to reach old age, which has, of course, cursed not a few millions of people with the loss of some physical and/or some mental abilities.

Indeed, as an unavoidable result of the inevitable loss of some physical and/or some mental abilities, many a man who has been alive for many years has become a boy again. In other words, not a few millions of parents strongly hope that their own children will step in by instantly becoming their own parents' foster parents, if and when the parents reach their second childhood. It goes without saying that in many if not most cases where the parent has managed to not only reach old age but also become their own child or children's foster child, their child or children also help them financially. That is, needless to say, one of the main real reasons why most parents move heaven and earth to give their children the best education they can.

In a nutshell, many a sane parent's relationship with their sane child is based on the following implicit command by the parent (which is, needless to say, based on the proverb *You scratch my back and I'll scratch yours*): "I'm scratching your back (for a decade or two) and (unless you are or will be a bad person or one of us will be dead then) you'll scratch mine (in three or so decades' time when it itches)."

The Pursuit of Meaningfulness

Although it is definitely possible to do so, the average sane parent, like pretty much all sane human beings over the age of six, seems incapable of maintaining their sanity throughout their involuntary walk from their mother's womb to the tomb that is eventually going to be fed their remains without using as a crutch the common belief that each and every human being's life has a purpose.

Having said that, that mental crutch alone, as far as I can see, is not enough to enable most human beings to maintain their sanity while they endure the recurrent pain of being alive and that of being sane. To the things that help most human beings in their daily endeavours to evade insanity, things such as the belief that each and every human being was born to play a particular earthly role that only they can play, we add many tiny goals and/or a few huge ones, and then we spend a huge portion of the remainder of our lives moving heaven and earth to dramatically increase our chances of eventually accomplishing those missions.

Bringing at least one child into this troubled world and then bringing them up is to many if not most sane parents one of the aforementioned goals, which many millions of sane human beings have chosen and now spend a significant portion of their lives pursuing. In other words, while the being that is apparently believed by a few billion sane human beings to be our creator has supposedly chosen the goals whose accomplishment the being in question is believed to pursue through the lives of each and every human being, and while millions of sane human beings have become parents also because they believe that that being has commanded all fertile people or all fertile believers to reproduce, millions of sane human beings who do not believe that the being in question exists have chosen to become parents even though they do not believe that we have to reproduce because the being in question—whose existence they deny—has commanded us to do so. Be that as it may, like most of those who do, many if not most of the sane parents who do not believe in the being in question were gradually persuaded or intimidated into adding parenthood to the goals that they are or were pursuing.

To sum up, parenthood gives many if not most sane parents what they believe is a valid reason for them to continue living even though this world of ours is without a doubt troubled. What's more, having children who are financially dependent on them definitely makes the dullness of most parents' jobs a little bit more bearable. It goes without saying that, in addition to other facts and misbeliefs, that, that is, being sincerely needed by someone else, makes many if not most sane parents, especially those who are taking care of their children, feel important.

The Evasion of Mortality

Needless to say, although the number of people who are occasionally or usually subjected to physical and/ or psychological pain is more than seven billion, the number of people who sincerely want to die someday is probably less than a tenth if not a hundredth of a million. That is as if or because Mother Nature has blessed or cursed nearly all sane human beings with a very strong desire to live forever. Unfortunately for most of us, and fortunately for some of us, we cannot live that long. As might have been expected, that has led to yet another use of children.

In a nutshell, because they had or have finally realized that their bodies cannot travel that far into the future, many if not most of us are or were each used by our own parent or parents as a desperate subconscious attempt of theirs to live until the end of time.

Before we decide whether or not to crucify those parents, we need to bear in mind that, in addition to not a few others, many if not most of them are or were used by their own parents to chase the very same thing. What's more, many if not most of us, the aforementioned parents' grandchildren, have used, are using, or will use our own children's existence to subconsciously chase the very same thing that our parents have subconsciously chased or are subconsciously chasing through our existence. In other words, among not a few others, many if not most of us have used, are using, or will use our own children's existence as a subconscious attempt of ours to throw our genes as far into the future as we possibly can, to send our genes to a very distant place called The Very Last Nanosecond of Existence, since our bodies are not durable enough to reach that far.

Speaking of genes, one of the real reasons why many a sane human being has intentionally become a parent is because they were curious to see what or who the baby that would spring from their womb or be conceived with the help of one of the many millions of cells that are produced by their testicles would look like.

The Ideal Human Being

Mental and Physical Disabilities

When it comes to human reproduction, all that Mother Nature wants is, I believe, for human beings to keep on producing human beings. It matters not to Her, I believe, whether or not the human beings that we are producing are or will someday be, as the politically correct say through euphemistic terms, mentally ill or physically challenged. And that, as far as I can see, is because, like many if not most human beings who are neither mentally nor physically disabled, many if not most human beings who are disabled are or will someday be able to reproduce. What's more, there are, as we all know, millions of people who are not and will never be able to reproduce despite the fact that they are neither mentally nor physically disabled.

Needless to say, one can, with reason, assert that, judging from Her attitude towards them, Society does not want disabled people. Or that, if one is to paint Her as less inhuman than She is, Society prefers abled people to disabled people.

Let us touch on mental illnesses before we remark on Society's attitude towards disabled people, particularly those whose disabilities are physical.

First things first, I do not, if truth be told, know much about mental illnesses despite the fact that I have had innumerable conversations with people who are classified as insane, and I have been called insane, wacko, mad, crazy, nuts, et cetera, et cetera, by not a few readers a few seconds, minutes, days, or even weeks after they had each read a few pages or even a single sentence that I have written.

Anyway, some people strongly believe that mental illness is a social construct—that is to say, an idea or notion that seems natural and obvious to people who accept it but may or may not represent reality, and therefore remains, to a great extent, an invention or artifice of a given society[55]. Among other points, some of them argue, in defense of that conviction, that "mental illnesses are simply behaviours that are not considered socially acceptable," and that terms such as *crazy*, *mentally ill*, *mad*, *mental*, *coo coo bananas*, and *bonkers*, "have been reduced to casual insults rather than real official medical terms."[56]

As far as I can see, the following are the main if not the only reasons why sane human beings are divided by the belief that mental illness is a social construct: One, most if not all thesauruses list terms such as *mad*, *crazy*, *mentally ill*, and *insane* as synonyms. And, two, conditions such as *anxiety disorders* (panic disorder, social anxiety disorder, specific phobias, etc.), *mood disorders* (depression, bipolar disorder, cyclothymic disorder, etc.), *psychotic disorders* (disorders that involve distorted awareness and thinking; e.g., *hallucination*, an experience involving the apparent perception of something not present, and *delusion*, an idiosyncratic belief or impression that is firmly maintained despite being contradicted by reality or rational argument)[57], and *eating disorders* (anorexia nervosa, bulimia nervosa, binge eating disorder, etc.) are recognized as mental illnesses.[58]

Believe it or not, if I were to be asked to take sides, I wouldn't. Instead of doing that, I would simply share the following relevant terms and their definitions: (1) *Psychosis* — a severe mental disorder in which thought and emotions are so impaired that contact is lost with external reality[59]; and (2) *Neurosis* — a relatively mild mental illness that is not caused by organic disease, involving symptoms of stress (depression, anxiety, obsessive behaviour, hypochondria) but not a radical loss of touch with reality.[60]

Let us now do what I have just promised the reader, namely, to touch on Society's attitude towards people who are physically disabled.

As I have already said, Mother Nature does not seem to have a problem with disabled people. I mean, She has never stopped making disabled people and making people disabled ever since She made the world's very first disabled person. Although I have absolutely no idea why She produces them, unlike many millions of people whose opposing belief was definitely coloured the most by Society, I do not believe that disabled people are useless factory rejects.

Firstly, many millions of disabled people are each older than their disability or disabilities. In other words, not every disabled person was born disabled. As a matter of fact, the most upsetting thing about Society's attitude towards disabled people is that many millions of disabled people became disabled while trying to please Society, the very same bitch that secretly regards them as subhuman. And, secondly, it is worth remembering that the usefulness and the uselessness of an individual is determined by (the needs and wants of) Society not (the needs and wants of) Mother Nature (who will eventually use most disabled people's bodies to achieve the very same thing that She will eventually use most abled people's bodies to achieve, because worms—unlike Society—do not discriminate against disabled people).

It goes without saying that many if not most abled people who hate and/or look down on disabled people do so merely because they, believe it or not, are of the unshakable belief that disabled people do not contribute to the economy. As far as I can see, that is a fallacy because even disabled children who cannot do anything except eat and drink have contributed to the growth of the economy when they increased, and they continue to contribute to that by increasing or at least maintaining, the amount of money that innumerable tax-paying grocery stores make each and every month from the families into which they were born. What's more, (1) there are innumerable other tax-paying businesses that would not be as profitable as they are if people who are disabled did not exist; (2) innumerable tax-paying individuals are employed by tax-paying companies whose products and services would without a doubt be worthless if there were no disabled people; and (3) innumerable people from whom innumerable tax-paying businesses make money regularly would be moneyless if they were not hired to look after disabled people.

To that one can, of course, add the undeniable fact that many millions of disabled people each contributes to the growth of the economy not only as a consumer but also as an employee ... or an employer (in innumerable cases, an employer whose employees are mostly or all abled). What's more, there are many millions of abled people who, like disabled people who cannot do anything except eat and drink, contribute to the growth of the economy only as consumers, even though they are still a few decades away from the average retirement age. Plus many of them have never paid income tax; and many of them will never pay it.

Even if we were to ignore their contribution as consumers, what would still make some of us doubt that some of the people who believe that disabled people do not contribute to the economy are over the age of six is, of course, the fact that within the group of people who are classified as disabled one finds people who are paraplegic or hemiplegic, amputees who have at least one hand, and people with only one malformed leg or arm. Obviously, in such a case the disability does not make it impossible for one to be an accountant, a writer, an actor, a teacher, an architect, a porn star, et cetera, et cetera. Morality aside, porn stars—like prostitutes—contribute way more to the life of the economy than many millions of people who are unemployed, many of whom are (or are merely regarded as) righteous. I mean, not only do porn stars and prostitutes contribute to the growth of the economy by using services that are provided, and by consuming products that are produced, by innumerable tax-paying businesses, they also provide services and produce products that are used and sometimes paid for by many millions of men ... women, boys, and girls, many if not most of whom are regarded as righteous by most if not all of the people who know them. (It is, I believe, worth noting that if it were not for their generally disapproved of livelihoods, innumerable porn stars and prostitutes would not, needless to say, have the money with which they regularly buy things, usually or always from businesses that usually or always pay tax. And, if they were not regularly having sex for and/or with strangers, many of them would have definitely starved to death). What's more, one can, of course, argue that pornography kills way fewer people than products that are made by companies such as Bavarian Motor Works, McDonald's, Heineken International, and Coca-Cola. And the same is probably true about prostitution.

(Speaking of the economy and prostitution, there is a modified aphorism of mine that is, I believe, worth sharing with the reader, namely, "'Prostitution' is a euphemism for rape incidents from which the victim and the economy profit.")

Be that as it may, one can argue, in defense of the aforementioned companies, that while their products have definitely led to innumerable people's deaths, they have also led to innumerable people's births. As I have recently quipped through an aphorism of mine, "Millions of human deaths would not have happened if it weren't for the consumption of alcohol. The same can be said about millions of human births." In other words, millions of dead people would be alive today if companies such as the aforementioned companies never existed. Having said that, many a man would not have been given the permission to insert his penis into the vagina of the woman who is now the mother of his child or children, if he did not drive a Beemer then; many a man, if he had not evaded the group that is made up of unemployed men by working at McDonald's; many a man, if he had not bought a Big Mac and a Coke for the woman; and many a man, if the few bottles of Heineken that he had consumed did not give him the fleeting courage to make a move on her.

Finally, I would like to conclude this part of our exploration by citing a few remarks that are said to have been made by Stella Young, who, as far as I can tell, was an Australian comedian, journalist, and disability rights activist: (1) "By far the most disabling thing in my life is the physical environment. It dictates what I can and can't do every day." (2) "The problem for many people with disabilities is not that we are not able to work a certain number of hours a week. It's that no one will let us." (3) "In Australia, a deaf per-

son attending an interview must take their own inter-
preter at their own expense, or ask the employer to
provide one. Believe me, nothing says 'I'm the best
person for this job' quite like asking an employer to
pay to interview you." and (4) "I use the term 'disabled people' quite deliberately, because I subscribe to
what's called the social model of disability, which tells
us that we are more disabled by the society that we
live in than by our bodies and our diagnoses."

Playing and Correcting God

This part is about the use of children by Society, which,
of course, we have already touched on. I have decided
to touch on this at this particular point of our exploration only because people with disabilities, like homosexuals and some racial or ethic groups, were among
the groups of people whose number some societies, or
rather some people who lived in some societies, once
endeavoured to reduce to zero.

I am, of course, referring to eugenics, that is to say,
the belief that or the practices that are rooted in the

belief that it is possible to improve the qualities of the human species or a human population, especially by such means as discouraging reproduction by persons having genetic defects or presumed to have inheritable undesirable traits (negative eugenics) or encouraging reproduction by persons presumed to have inheritable desirable traits (positive eugenics).[61]

Let us touch on the former. In the first decades of the twentieth century, for example, more than 30 American states adopted compulsory sterilization laws, which apparently led to the sterilization of over 60,000 "disabled" people, many of whom were involuntarily sterilized because they were mentally disabled or ill, or because they lived on the margins of society and belonged to groups that are or were socially disadvantaged. Naturally, not a few people believe that that has influenced the National Socialist compulsory sterilization program, which is said to have led to about 350,000 compulsory sterilizations between 1934 and 1945 and is believed to have been a stepping stone to the mass murder of Jews under the German Nazi regime between 1941 and 1945,[62] a period during which, according to *New Oxford American*

Dictionary, more than 6 million European Jews, as well as members of other persecuted groups such as gypsies and homosexuals, were murdered at concentration camps such as Auschwitz.

In closing, I would like to share two relevant remarks. The first is said to have been made by Charles Eliot; the second, by Oliver Wendell Holmes: (1) "Society must concern itself not chiefly with the isolation, temporary or permanent, of the individual murderer, thief, or forger, but with the extermination or repair of the genetic, educational, or industrial defects which cause the production of criminals." and (2) "It is better for all the world if, instead of waiting to execute degenerate offspring for crime or to let them starve for their imbecility, society can prevent those who are manifestly unfit from continuing their kind.... Three generations of imbeciles are enough."[63]

Abortion, Suicide, Homosexuality, and Masturbation

Needless to say, every single one of those issues has

had and continues to have a significant impact on the size of the human population, especially the first two.

In a nutshell, as I have asserted in a satirical essay of mine titled "On Masturbation," like homosexuality, masturbation is in a way a threat to the institution of the (nuclear) family, which is, of course, a basic social unit that is made up of parents and their children and is one of the main things that Society uses in the socialization process, which is Society's never-ending endeavour to, among other things, mold each and every one of as many sane children as She possibly can into what is to Her an Ideal Citizen, that is to say, a creature that is subservient to the state and the church, a creature that dare not question whatever it is fed and the arrogant claims that are made by its political and its religious leaders.

Of course, homosexuality and masturbation, unlike suicide and abortion, do not end human lives; they merely prevent the production of children, products that, as I have asserted earlier, Society needs to continuously produce by begging or forcing us to reproduce in order for Her to continue to evade senility, which could, of course, eventually lead to Her own death. In the nature of things, while She is without a doubt hostile to all four of them, Society is ten times less hostile to homosexuality (because She strongly believes that the vast majority of human beings are not homosexual) and a thousand times less hostile to masturbation (because She is of the unshakable belief that most of the people who masturbate are heterosexual and are each therefore a biological parent or a trillion times more likely to become one than all homosexuals) than She is towards suicide and abortion.

To be sure, the reader could justifiably argue that sometimes homosexuality leads to human death, since innumerable people were killed for being homosexual. Having said that, I would readily shatter that argument into a few trillion pieces by simply reminding the reader that the people who were unfortunately killed for being homosexual were not killed by their sexual attraction to people of their own sex; they were killed by people who have or had a problem with that. In other words, homosexuals who were killed because of their sexual orientation were killed by homophobic people; they were not killed by homosexuality or homophobia.

Childless versus Childfree

As we all know, there are innumerable sane people who became parents unintentionally and, needless to say, countless sane people who have decided not to become parents. (I might be wrong, but I strongly believe that the number of people who fall under the first group is hundreds of thousands if not millions of times more than that of those who belong to the second.)

Although the meanings of those suffixes—"-less" and "-free"—are sometimes the same ("free from"), the meanings and, perhaps more important, the connotations of *childless* and *childfree* are usually if not always different: *childless* simply means "without children," whereas *childfree* is used to refer to people who chose not to have children, that is, to tell the reader or the listener that such a person's lack of a child is by choice not temporary or imposed on them by things such as infertility—obviously, one can (decide to) become a parent after having decided to never become one; if one is still fertile, that is. Indeed, that is the main reason why many if not most of the people who are childfree loathe being referred to as childless: they believe that the "-less" in "childless" implies that they lack something that they want or need, namely, a child.

While that is without a doubt likely to seem like a distinction without a difference to some people, especially people who have children and people who do not and cannot have children, that distinction has had and will always have a significant impact on the size of the human population and, as a result, a significant impact on each and every human being's chances of not dying from starvation. I mean, in addition to dramatically decreasing the number of people who feel sorry for people who are childfree (that is, people who *chose* not to have children) for not having children, that distinction has dramatically increased the number of people who, when they are dead, will have managed to resist the social, cultural, and/or religious pressure to reproduce. In other words, that seemingly unnecessary distinction, which definitely tells or reminds one that there are many people who chose not to have children, has, as far as I can see, given and will give innumerable people the strength and the courage required to remain childfree.

Interestingly, there are people who loathe the term *childfree*. "I have ... antipathy for the term *childfree*; it seems to me to imply that children are a burden, something to be avoided. Think about words like *drug-free* or *worry-free*; just as the suffix *-less* implies that you are missing out on something good or necessary, the suffix *-free* implies that you are avoiding something bad."[64]

Anyway, another interesting fact, which is relevant to not only the topic in question but also the one that I am about to touch on, is that many if not most parents strongly believe that people who have decided not to have children are selfish, whereas many if not most of the people who have decided not to have children are of the unshakable belief that making a baby on purpose is a selfish act. In addition to that, many if not most sane people who are no longer children strongly believe that people who have decided not to have children will eventually regret their decision when it is too late for them to become parents.

Finally, it is, I believe, worth mentioning that not every childfree person hates children. Many if not most of the people who are childfree actually love and enjoy children. Unlike most people who became parents intentionally, they just don't believe that parenthood is a prerequisite for loving and enjoying children.

Antinatalism

Another fact that is worth mentioning is that people who are childfree are not necessarily antinatalists. As I have just said, many of them actually love and enjoy children; unlike many if not most parents, they just don't believe that one needs to own a child in order for one to be able to love and to enjoy the child. (I beg the alert reader to refuse to allow those two sentences to deceive the reader into believing that I believe that all antinatalists hate and/or do not enjoy children.)

This exploration of ours would, I believe, be incomplete without touching on anti-natalism, owing to the fact that it is, of course, the antithesis of natalism (also called pro-natalism), which, needless to say, we have already touched on.

As might have been expected, there are people who, in addition to being opposed to both the religious and the secular promotion of human reproduction, are strongly opposed to human reproduction itself. Those people are, of course, called antinatalists, which obviously means that that term is another way of referring to adherents of antinatalism. In other words, antinatalism is a philosophy that strives to reduce the size of the human population to zero, and therefore encourages the prevention of and disapproves of human reproduction.

There are at least four kinds of antinatalism, namely, ecological antinatalism, teleological antinatalism, philanthropic antinatalism, and misanthropic antinatalism. As an attempt to shatter the wrong impression that the last sentence of the last paragraph will give many a reader, let us touch on only two: (1) *Misanthropic antinatalism* — produces people who discourage and disapprove of human reproduction because they want to reduce the size of the human population to zero because they dislike or hate human beings; and (2) *Philanthropic antinatalism* — produces people who discourage and disapprove of human reproduction because they want to reduce the size of the human population to zero because they like or love human beings, people whose controversial goal is to bring about the extinction of human beings in order to prevent the countless trillions of instances of physical pain and the innumerable trillions of instances of mental pain that will without a doubt someday be unequally distributed among "human beings" who are not yet conceived; as Arthur Schopenhauer is said to have written in *On the Sufferings of the World*, "If children were brought into the world by an act of pure reason alone, would the human race continue to exist? Would not a man rather have so much sympathy with the coming generation as to spare it the burden of existence, or at any rate not take it upon himself to impose that burden upon it in cold blood?"

Childlessness and Selfishness

I would like to begin this penultimate part of this exploration of ours by sharing a conviction of mine as to who is right between the aforementioned parents who strongly believe that people who are childfree are selfish and childfree people who are of the unshakable belief that parents who have brought children into this world intentionally are selfish: In a word, I strongly believe that both parties are right ... and wrong. They are each right in thinking that people who belong to the other group are selfish, and wrong in thinking that they are not selfish.

Although that is certainly not one of the reasons why I penned it or this book, this third and last part of this book substantiates a relevant conviction of mine on which a satirical essay of mine titled "The Selfish Genie" is based, namely, all human beings are selfish. Because I am an avid student of general semantics, I, in that essay, tell the reader that by "selfish" I mean "concerned *primarily* with one's own personal profit or pleasure" not "lacking consideration for others."

As the reader may have already noticed, like Society, many a company, Mother Nature, and every single country, each and every person whose use of a child or children we have just touched on has used or is using the child or children primarily for his or her own personal profit or pleasure not that of the child or children who they have used or are using. What's more, in countless cases the children do not or did not benefit at all, and, sad to say, in innumerable cases the children were harmed (girls who were raped by men who raped them in order to "cure" themselves of HIV are, of course, a great example) and/or eventually killed (some premature deaths, for example, were caused by diseases that were caused by regular consumption of junk food, which, according to some people, kills way more people than wars, genocide, and famine … combined[65]).

Companies that sell junk food, for example, sell junk food primarily if not only because they want to make money. Such companies are a great example because most if not all of their shareholders know that in many millions of instances regular consumption of junk food, which they are forever looking for new ways to make even more addictive, has caused diseases that are deadly.

Speaking of death, allow me to touch on our attitude towards abortion and suicide in order to further substantiate my conviction that we are all selfish. Unlike the selfishness of people who are against abortion and those who are against suicide, the selfishness of people who have deliberately terminated their own lives and/or the lives of the embryos or fetuses that were developing inside their wombs is self-evident. Let us focus only on people who are against suicide. In a word, we are against people killing themselves, primarily if not only because their deaths would instantly or eventually disadvantage or hurt *us* (directly or indirectly) and/or because *we* would no longer get the things that *we* are getting from them; or *we* would have to look for new sources, that is to say, people from whom *we* would get those things. Obviously, most of us are not honest enough to admit and/or smart enough to realize that.

Finally, while I am about to share them only to substantiate another conviction of mine, which I am about to share, the following expressions of regret and disappointment also substantiate my conviction that we human beings are selfish, we are each concerned primarily with our own personal profit or pleasure.

Negative Reviews of a Product Called Child

It goes without saying that there are gazillions of parents who are sincerely happy that they are parents, even though their being parents has dramatically increased the number of times they worry and the number of things they worry about. And that that includes innumerable parents who became parents way earlier than they had planned and countless parents who had decided to never become parents.

In addition to the fact that doing that is made unnecessary by the previous paragraph, the reason why I will not share any positive reviews is because it is, needless to say, pretty much impossible to tell with absolute certainty whether a parent who claims that he or she loves parenthood really loves being a parent. (As we all know, most sane human beings who are over the age of six usually act or react not as per what they genuinely feel or really think but in accordance with the expectations of those around them: chances are that in a society that is made up of five sane adults, person A's sincere or fake happiness will inspire person B to fake happiness; person B's fake happiness will then fill person C and person D with an irresistible urge to pretend to be happy; and then, as soon as he or she is under the impression that everyone around him or her is happy, person E will move heaven and earth to speak or act in a manner with which he or she will attempt to give as many people as he or she can the impression that he or she is happy. Moreover, being a parent is to many if not most parents what being a smoker is to many if not most smokers: something they became because of peer pressure, and then they each stole or came up with a reason or reasons with which they sometimes justify their being that and/ or a lie or lies with regard to why they became that.) What's more, even if and especially when it is shared anonymously, a negative review of this kind of a product is a trillion times more unlikely than a positive one to be untruthful.

Here goes: (1) "I secretly hate being a mother. I never wanted to be pregnant or ever have children, but I'm a ******* idiot and had careless sex with my ex. Now I feel trapped in a relationship with him and with a child I secretly wish I never had. My dream was to travel the world and focus on my career, now I'm

stuck with a man who is all about himself, who is boring, has no ambition, lazy, depressed, and manipu-
lative. Sometimes I wish I had the balls to just leave
him. Sometimes I wish religion wasn't a factor in my
life so I could have had an abortion and continued on
the right path I was once on."[66] (2) "I don't like being a
mother. I dread waking in the morning knowing I will
try to get ready for work with him screaming. I dread
coming home from work and picking him up; finding
food he will eat and not throw on the floor; keeping
him from breaking everything. I look forward to bed-
time, only to cry when he refuses to sleep, even though
he is exhausted. And then it all starts over again.... I
have no idea who I am. There is no time for me."[67] (3)
"I love my daughter more than anything else in the
world, but she just needs so much from me. I wasn't
ready for this, I had no idea how much of a drain it
would be on me.... We hardly ever have sex because
our daughter has nightmares and we leave our door
open at night in case she gets scared. I really miss being able to just take off on fun trips without having to
worry about dragging her along or finding someone
to take care of her while we're away. Constantly wor-

rying about her health, safety, and wellbeing makes me want to pull every last hair out of my head and collapse into a heap on the floor. There are too many things to consider and I just want to have a good time. I'm just not okay with giving as much of myself as a child demands. Why did I do this?... Every now and then I fantasize about abandoning my family and starting a new life somewhere that people don't need me. I would never follow through with that, and I always feel awful about it, but it helps me get through bad days."[68] (4) "I'm a Christian and I had my child because I was taught that it was wrong to have an abortion. I love my son. He is so beautiful. But I hate being a mother. I'm a single mother with very little support. It's really hard. Everyone feels for the children but no one cares for the mothers. We have to put on this fake facade of being a contented mother when inside we're miserable."[69] (5) "In my heart of hearts, I don't like being a mother. I love my children, I do, and I write these words anonymously so they never find out the horrible feelings I feel. But I have to get them off of my chest somehow; the burden has become too much to bear. Ever since becoming a mother 12 years ago, and every day since, I haven't been able to escape the sinking feeling that I shouldn't be one. It's not the trivial things that people complain about like peeing with an audience or having to drive to endless lacrosse games. It's the fact that I truly liked my life better before I was a parent. I liked *who I was* better, and I spend an inordinate amount of time dreaming of those days. I take good care of my children and they have an adoring father, grandparents and aunts and uncles. They are well adjusted, happy human beings. They are fine. It's me who's the problem. Me who feels like I'm playing a role I wasn't meant to play every single day of my life. Me who must be missing some chain of DNA that all mothers are supposed to possess. I'm sure I'll be called a bad parent and people will suggest I just leave home, that my kids would be better off without me. But I won't, because I don't think I can *ever* truly be happy again, whether I'm at home with two kids or living on my own somewhere far away. Guilt would consume me either way, so I may as well be the only one to suffer and not bring the whole family down with me. And there's always nighttime, when the kids are soundly sleeping and I can dream of the days before motherhood; the days that should have lasted forever."[70] (6) "I don't enjoy being a mom either. From my point of view my husband doesn't respect me for that choice. I did it for him not for me. I hate the tantrums, the questions about where's my laundry, or the guilt if I don't want to pick up behind him. I hate it all.... As I am writing this I am angry, angry that a mom should feel guilty for expressing the truth.... I so understand why divorce happens."[71] (7) "I fucking hate being a mum. There I've said it. I have completely lost my identity and life. I am at the bottom of the list of priorities in my home.... I am so tired. I went out on Saturday for the fourth time in nearly 2 years. I am so fucking resentful of my daughter sometimes and I hate myself for it because obviously she is completely innocent and undeserving of this."[72] (8) "I don't think I ever had cause to use the word 'drudgery' before I became a mother. Now it's a very important piece of my vocabulary because it describes what I do every day."[73] (9) "I hate, hate, hate being a mom. I hate every moment of it and that I have to put on a happy face because I can't tell anyone how much I dislike this part of my life.... I applaud those who wrote truth. Thank you for giving me the courage to stand up and say 'we love our kids, but we hate the job!'"[74] (10) "I hate being a parent on almost every single level. I love my daughter and will do anything for her... I saw friends growing up become shadows of what they once were after their kids were born. Once happy people are now broken, miserable individuals who hate what their lives have become but put on a happy face to keep themselves from becoming pariahs.... I hate what my life has become... And yes, we can be great parents and still hate what our lives have become. Having children is not rewarding in the least, and at best it is an inescapable prison. When she's old enough, I can only hope that we hid our resentment well enough for her to be successful in life. And our best piece of advice to her will be to get her tubes tied so she never has to experience the miserable existence of parenthood. Go out, enjoy life, and don't get saddled by kids. I won't be unhappy to not be a grandparent... and I've already scheduled a vasectomy to ensure this travesty never happens a second time to my already intolerable life.... I'll be damned if my daughter suffers because of my personal feelings. One day when she's old enough to understand, I'll explain to her the absolute and concentrated horror that is parenthood."[75]

Indeed, the parents who were kind enough to anonymously share those remarks have given us a once-in-a-lifetime opportunity to see what is concealed by the masks that are always worn by innumerable parents whose actions and remarks have left most if not all of the people who know them with the unshakable belief that those parents love and enjoy parenthood. It goes without saying that, because we sane human beings are such great actors, in many if not most of the cases such as the aforecited cases the group of people who have been deceived into believing and still believe that the parent loves and enjoys being a parent includes not only the parent's child or children but also the person with whom the parent has brought the child or children into this world into which we have all been brought without our permission; a troubled world into which we were each brought either unintentionally, or primarily or even only for the sake of Society and/or our parents ... or parent.

MOKOKOMA MOKHONOANA

Other published writings

To browse other books and essays by Mokokoma, visit *mokokoma.com* (each book or essay is listed with links to some retailers from whom you can buy it).

Be one of the first to know

For the most convenient and less noisy way to follow his work, simply subscribe to his newsletter at *mokokoma.com*. Other than an occasional link to a new book, essay, cartoon, or design his newsletters are made up of nothing but his new aphorisms, which, if you subscribe, you will get *a week or two before he shares them anywhere.* Your email address will never be shared with anyone, and you can unsubscribe at any time. The maximum number of newsletters you will receive in a month is four; the minimum is zero.

Liked a few things in this book?

If you found this book worthy of your precious time, please consider leaving a review, even if it is made up of a single sentence. That seemingly insignificant gesture will immensely help Mokokoma and, more important, some, many, or even most of the people who your review will have persuaded to read this book.

REFERENCES

THE IDEA OF CHILDHOOD

1. Postman, Neil. *The Disappearance of Childhood.* New York: Vintage Books, 1994., p. xii.
2. Ibid., xi.
3. Ibid.
4. Ibid., p. xii.
5. Ibid., p. xi.
6. Ibid., p. 10.
7. Ibid., p. 16.
8. Ibid., p. 17.
9. Ibid., p. 10.
10. Ibid., p. 11.
11. Ibid., p. 12.

12. Ibid., p. 15.
13. Ibid., p. 18.
14. Ibid., p. 14.
15. Ibid., p. 20.
16. Ibid., p. 36.
17. Ibid., p. 72.
18. Ibid.
19. Ibid., p. 84.
20. Ibid., p. 77.
21. Ibid., p. 78.
22. Ibid., p. 79.
23. Ibid., p. 84.
24. Ibid., p. 85.
25. Ibid.
26. Ibid., p. 86.

THE HUMAN USE OF CHILDREN

1. Schlesinger, Rudolf. *The Family in the USSR*. New York: Routledge, 1949., p. 372.
2. Eke, Steven. "Russia faces demographic disaster." BBC.co.uk. http://news.bbc.co.uk/2/hi/

europe/5056672.stm (Accessed April 21, 2017).

3. The Associated Press. "Baby, and a car! Russians hold conception day." NBCNEWS.com. http://www.nbcnews.com/id/20730526/ns/world_news-europe/t/baby-car-russians-hold-conception-day (Accessed April 21, 2017).

4. Levine, Yasha. "Incentivized Birth: How Russia's baby-boosting policies are hurting the population." Slate.com. http://www.slate.com/articles/news_and_politics/dispatches/2008/07/incentivized_birth.html (Accessed April 21, 2017).

5. Wikimedia Foundation, Inc. "fallacy of composition." Wikipedia.org. https://en.wikipedia.org/wiki/Fallacy_of_composition (Accessed April 22, 2017).

6. Oxford University Press. "Power." OxfordDictionaries.com. https://en.oxforddictionaries.com/definition/power (accessed April 22, 2017).

7. "Colonialism vs Imperialism." IfCompare.com. http://www.ifcompare.com/colonialism-vs-imperialism (Accessed June 22, 2016).

8. Fromm, Erich. *To Have or to Be?*. New York: Continuum, 2010., p. 91.

9. Avila, Oscar. "Why settle for a polluted planet?" ChicagoTribune.com. http://articles.chicagotribune.com/2007-12-13/news/0712120903_1_cellulosic-polluted-fossil-fuels (Accessed April 24, 2017).

10. Fromm, Erich. *Escape from Freedom*. New York: Henry Holt and Company, 1994., p. 160.

11. Kennedy, Robert F. "Remarks at the University of Kansas, March 18, 1968." JfkLibrary.org. http://www.jfklibrary.org/Research/Research-Aids/Ready-Reference/RFK-Speeches/Remarks-of-Robert-F-Kennedy-at-the-University-of-Kansas-March-18-1968.aspx (Accessed August 1, 2016).

12. "Beyond GDP: Measuring progress, true wealth, and well-being." Europa.eu. http://ec.europa.eu/environment/beyond_gdp/key_quotes_en.html (Accessed April 29, 2017).

13. Northstar22. "Why Does Religion Promote Procreation?" City-Data.com. http://www.city-data.com/forum/religion-spirituality/1170479-why-does-religion-promote-procreation.html (Accessed May 1, 2017).

14. Moesker, J. "Family Planning and Birth Control."

ChristianStudyLibrary.org. http://www.christi-anstudylibrary.org/files/pub/20110231%20-%20Moesker%20J%20-%20Family%20Planning%20and%20Birth%20Control.pdf (Accessed May 1, 2017).

15. McKeown, John. *God's Babies: Natalism and Bible Interpretation in Modern America*. Open-Book Publishers, 2014., p. 50.

16. International Labour Organization. "Child Labour In Gold Mining." Ilo.org. http://www.ilo.org/ipec/areas/Miningandquarrying/Moreabout-CLinmining/lang--en/index.htm (Accessed May 4, 2017).

17. Make Chocolate Fair! "Cocoa production in a nut-shell." MakeChocolateFair.org. http://makechoc-olatefair.org/issues/cocoa-production-nutshell (Accessed May 4, 2017).

18. Ibid.

19. Lamb, Christina. "The Child Slaves of the Ivory Coast - Bought and Sold for as Little as £40." Telegraph.co.uk. http://www.telegraph.co.uk/news/worldnews/africaandindianocean/cotedivoire/1317006/The-child-slaves-of-the-

Ivory-Coast-bought-and-sold-for-as-little-as-40.
html (Accessed May 4, 2017).

20. Global Exchange. "Film Shows Cocoa Child
Slavery Continues." GlobalExchange.org.
http://www.globalexchange.org/blogs/
fairtrade/2010/08/04/film-shows-cocoa-child-
slavery-continues (Accessed May 4, 2017).

21. United States Department of Labor. "Child Labor
and Forced Labor Reports." Dol.gov. https://
www.dol.gov/agencies/ilab/resources/reports/
child-labor/cote-divoire (Accessed May 5, 2017).

22. Kramer, Anna. "Women and the Big Business of
Chocolate." OxfamAmerica.org. https://www.
oxfamamerica.org/explore/stories/women-and-
the-big-business-of-chocolate-1 (Accessed May 5,
2017).

23. Hawksley, Humphrey. "Ivory Coast Accuses
Chocolate Companies." BBC.co.uk. http://news.
bbc.co.uk/2/hi/africa/1311982.stm (Accessed
May 5, 2017).

24. Lamb, Christina. "The Child Slaves of the
Ivory Coast - Bought and Sold for As Little As
£40." Telegraph.co.uk. http://www.telegraph.

co.uk/news/worldnews/africaandindianocean/
cotedivoire/1317006/The-child-slaves-of-the-
Ivory-Coast-bought-and-sold-for-as-little-as-40.
html (Accessed May 6, 2017).

25. Food Empowerment Project. "Child Labor and
Slavery in the Chocolate Industry." Foodispower.
org. http://www.foodispower.org/slavery-choco-
late (Accessed May 6, 2017).

26. McMahon, Kate. "AFRICA: The Dark Side of
Chocolate." CorpWatch.org. http://www.corp-
watch.org/article.php?id=12754 (Accessed May
8, 2017).

27. Morran, Chris. "Creator Of 'Your Baby Can
Read' Program Settles False Advertising Charges." Consumerist.com. https://consumerist.
com/2014/08/22/creator-of-your-baby-can-
read-program-settles-false-advertising-charges
(Accessed May 9, 2017).

28. Federal Trade Commission Washington, DC
20554. "Complaint and Request for Investiga-
tion and Relief." CommercialFreeChildhood.org.
http://www.commercialfreechildhood.org/sites/
default/files/ybcrftccomplaint.pdf (Accessed May

9, 2017).

29. Campaign for a Commercial-Free Childhood. "Your Baby Still Can't Read." SalsaLabs.com. http://org.salsalabs.com/o/621/p/dia/action3/common/public/?action_KEY=19405 (Accessed May 9, 2017).

30. Gordon, James. "Your Baby CAN'T Read!" DailyMail.co.uk. http://www.dailymail.co.uk/news/article-2742357/Your-baby-CAN-T-read-Firm-claimed-toddlers-reading-Harry-Potter-novels-age-three-fined-185-million-false-advertising.html (Accessed May 9, 2017).

31. Morra, Chris. "Creator Of "Your Baby Can Read" Program Settles False Advertising Charges." Consumerist.com. https://consumerist.com/2014/08/22/creator-of-your-baby-can-read-program-settles-false-advertising-charges (Accessed May 9, 2017).

32. Campaign for a Commercial-Free Childhood. "Your Baby Still Can't Read!" Commercial-FreeChildhood.org. http://www.commercialfreechildhood.org/action/your-baby-still-cant-read (Accessed May 9, 2017).

33. WebMD, Inc. "Beware These Empty Calories!" WebMD.com. http://www.webmd.com/diet/features/beware-empty-calories (Accessed May 9, 2017).

34. WebMD, Inc. "Health Risks Linked to Obesity." WebMD.com. http://www.webmd.com/diet/obesity/obesity-health-risks (Accessed May 11, 2017).

35. Bakalar, Nicholas. "Obesity Is Linked to at Least 13 Types of Cancer." NYTimes.com. https://well.blogs.nytimes.com/2016/08/24/obesity-linked-to-at-least-13-types-of-cancer (Accessed May 11, 2017).

36. York, Emily Bryson. "McDonald's Pulls Ads From Florida Report Cards." AdAge.com. http://adage.com/article/news/mcdonald-s-pulls-ads-florida-report-cards/123176 (Accessed May 12, 2017).

37. Elliott, Stuart. "Straight A's, With a Burger as a Prize." NYTimes.com. http://www.nytimes.com/2007/12/06/business/media/06adco.html (Accessed May 12, 2017).

38. Melissa. "10 Breakfast Cereals to Avoid." CARE2.com. http://www.care2.com/greenliving/10-breakfast-cereals-to-avoid.html (Accessed May

12, 2017).

39. HEALTHYCURES. "One Of The MOST TOXIC Cereals That You SHOULD NOT Be Feeding Your Child." HealthyCures.org. http://healthycures. org/cheerios-the-awful-truth-about-americas-favorite-cereal (Accessed May 12, 2017).

40. Amazon.com, Inc. "The Oreo Cookie Counting Book." Amazon.com. https://www.amazon.com/ Oreo-Cookie-Counting-Book/dp/0689834896 (Accessed May 13, 2017).

41. Campaign for a Commercial-Free Childhood. "Stop McTeacher's Nights Action Center." CommercialFreeChildhood.org. http://www.commercialfreechildhood.org/action/stopmcteachers-nights (Accessed May 13, 2017).

42. Cozens, Claire. "Cadbury Rethinks School Sports Initiative." TheGuardian.com. https://www.theguardian.com/media/2003/dec/03/advertising. marketingandpr (Accessed May 15, 2017).

43. The Food Commission. "Cadbury Wants Children to Eat Two Million Kg of Fat — to Get Fit." FoodComm.org.uk. http://www.foodcomm.org.uk/ articles/cadbury_in_schools (Accessed May 15,

2017).

44. Brown, Elizabeth. "Different Words for Sugar on Food Labels." SFGATE.com. http://healthyeating.sfgate.com/different-words-sugar-food-labels-8373.html (Accessed May 15, 2017).

45. Pikul, Corrie. "Is Juice Worse For You Than Soda?" HuffingtonPost.com. http://www.huffingtonpost.com/2014/05/07/is-juice-worse-than-soda_n_5213628.html (Accessed May 15, 2017).

46. Magee, Elaine. "Sugar Shockers: Foods Surprisingly High in Sugar." WebMD.com. http://www.webmd.com/food-recipes/features/sugar-shockers-foods-surprisingly-high-in-sugar (Accessed May 15, 2017).

47. American Heart Association, Inc. "Children Should Eat Less Than 25 Grams of Added Sugars Daily." Heart.org. http://newsroom.heart.org/news/children-should-eat-less-than-25-grams-of-added-sugars-daily (Access May 15, 2017).

48. The Coca-Cola Company. "Our Products." Coca-ColaProductFacts.com. http://www.coca-colaproductfacts.com/en/coca-cola-products/coca-cola (Accessed May 15, 2017).

49. United States Department of Agriculture Agricultural Research Service. "Basic Report: 19159, Candies, MARS SNACKFOOD US, 3 MUSKETEERS Bar." USDA.gov. https://ndb.nal.usda.gov/ndb/search/list?qlookup=19159 (Accessed May 15, 2017).

50. Wm. Wrigley Jr. Company. "U.S. Nutrition Information." Wrigley.com. http://www.wrigley.com/global/brands/nutrition.aspx (Accessed May 15, 2017).

51. O'Neil, Dennis. "Socialization." Palomar.edu. http://anthro.palomar.edu/social/soc_1.htm (Accessed May 17, 2017).

52. Syiasha. "Presentation Bullying." Scribd.com. https://www.scribd.com/document/7882659/Presentation-Bullying (Accessed May 17, 2017).

53. Brauns, Chris. "The Meaning of Proverbs 17:6 – On the Beauty of Grandchildren." ChrisBrauns.com. http://chrisbrauns.com/2013/07/proverbs-17-verse-6-the-beauty-of-grandchildren (Accessed May 17, 20).

54. Noxparadox1. "Do you ever seriously regret having kids? If so, why?" Reddit.com. https://www.

reddit.com/r/AskReddit/comments/1ayey7/par-
ents_of_reddit_do_you_ever_seriously_regret/
c91zhv1 (Accessed May 22, 2017).

55. Encyclopedia.com. "Social Constructs." Encyclo-
pedia.com. http://www.encyclopedia.com/social-
sciences/applied-and-social-sciences-magazines/
social-constructs (Accessed May 26, 2017).

56. Debatewise.org. "Is mental 'illness' socially con-
structed?" Debatewise.org. http://debatewise.
org/debates/1543-is-mental-illness-socially-con-
structed (Accessed May 26, 2017).

57. Oxford University Press. "Delusion." Oxford-
dictionaries.com. https://en.oxforddictionaries.
com/definition/delusion (Accessed May 26,
2017).

58. WebMD, LLC. "Types of Mental Illness." Web-
MD.com. http://www.webmd.com/mental-
health/mental-health-types-illness (Accessed
May 26, 2017).

59. Oxford University Press. "Psychosis." Oxford-
Dictionaries.com. https://en.oxforddictionaries.
com/definition/psychosis (Accessed May 29,
2017).

60. Oxford University Press. "Neurosis." Oxford-Dictionaries.com. https://en.oxforddictionaries.com/definition/neurosis (Accessed May 29, 2017).

61. Dictionary.com, LLC. "Eugenics." Dictionary.com. http://www.dictionary.com/browse/eugenics (Accessed May 31, 2017).

62. Kaelber, Lutz. "Eugenics: Compulsory Sterilization in 50 American States." Uvm.edu. https://www.uvm.edu/~lkaelber/eugenics (Accessed May 31, 2017).

63. Cornell Law School. "Buck v. Bell." Cornell.edu. https://www.law.cornell.edu/supremecourt/text/274/200 (Accessed May 31, 2017).

64. K, Sam. "Childless, Childfree, What's In A Name?" Wordpress.com. https://coolchildfree-guy.wordpress.com/2012/05/30/childless-child-free-whats-in-a-name/#comment-274 (Accessed May 31, 2017).

65. Wellmann, Jan."Junk Food Kills More Than Wars, Famine, Genocide." Honeycolony.com. https://www.honeycolony.com/article/junk-food-kills-more-than-war (Accessed June 1,

2017).

66. Jamie. "Hate Being a Mom." Secret-Confessions. com. http://www.secret-confessions.com/hate/ hate-being-a-mom#comment-37277 (Accessed June 2, 2017).

67. Me. "What if You Hate Being a Mom?" Mommy-wise.com. http://mommywise.com/hate-being-a-mom/#comment-8 (Accessed June 2, 2017).

68. Thrwymom. "I Hate Being a Mother." Reddit. com. https://www.reddit.com/r/offmychest/ comments/2b4aq8/i_hate_being_a_mother (Accessed June 2, 2017).

69. Wendy. "Hate being a mom." Secret-Confessions. com. http://www.secret-confessions.com/hate/ hate-being-a-mom#comment-4166 (Accessed June 2, 2017).

70. Anonymous. "I Don't Like Being a Mother." ScaryMommy.com. http://www.scarymommy. com/i-dont-like-being-a-mother (Accessed June 2, 2017).

71. Franklin, Portia. "What if You Hate Being a Mom?" Mommywise.com. http://mommywise. com/hate-being-a-mom/#comment-136 (Ac-

cessed June 2, 2017).

72. Gokwancarr. "I Fucking Hate Being a Mum." Mumsnet.com. https://www.mumsnet.com/Talk/parenting/752416-i-fucking-hate-being-a-mum (Accessed June 2, 2017).

73. Deemee. "I Love My Children but Hate Being a Mother ." Mumsnet.com. https://https://www.mumsnet.com/Talk/parenting/a1458875-I-love-my-children-but-hate-being-a-mother-does-anyone-feel-the-same-I-need-help (Accessed June 2, 2017).

74. Whatever. "Hate being a mom." Secret-Confessions.com. http://www.secret-confessions.com/hate/hate-being-a-mom#comment-4495 (Accessed June 2, 2017).

75. Anonymous. "Hate being a mom." Secret-Confessions.com. http://www.secret-confessions.com/hate/hate-being-a-mom#comment-17409 (Accessed June 2, 2017).

www.ingramcontent.com/pod-product-compliance
Lightning Source LLC
Chambersburg PA
CBHW021050090426
42738CB00006B/269